The Gold Rush

SOUTH DAKOTA

HISTORICAL SOCIETY

PRESS

Pierre

Black Hills History Tours

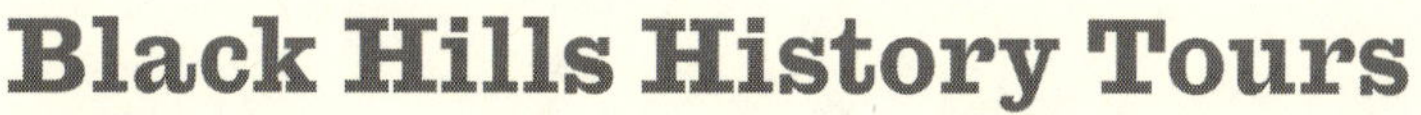

The Gold Rush

David A. Wolff

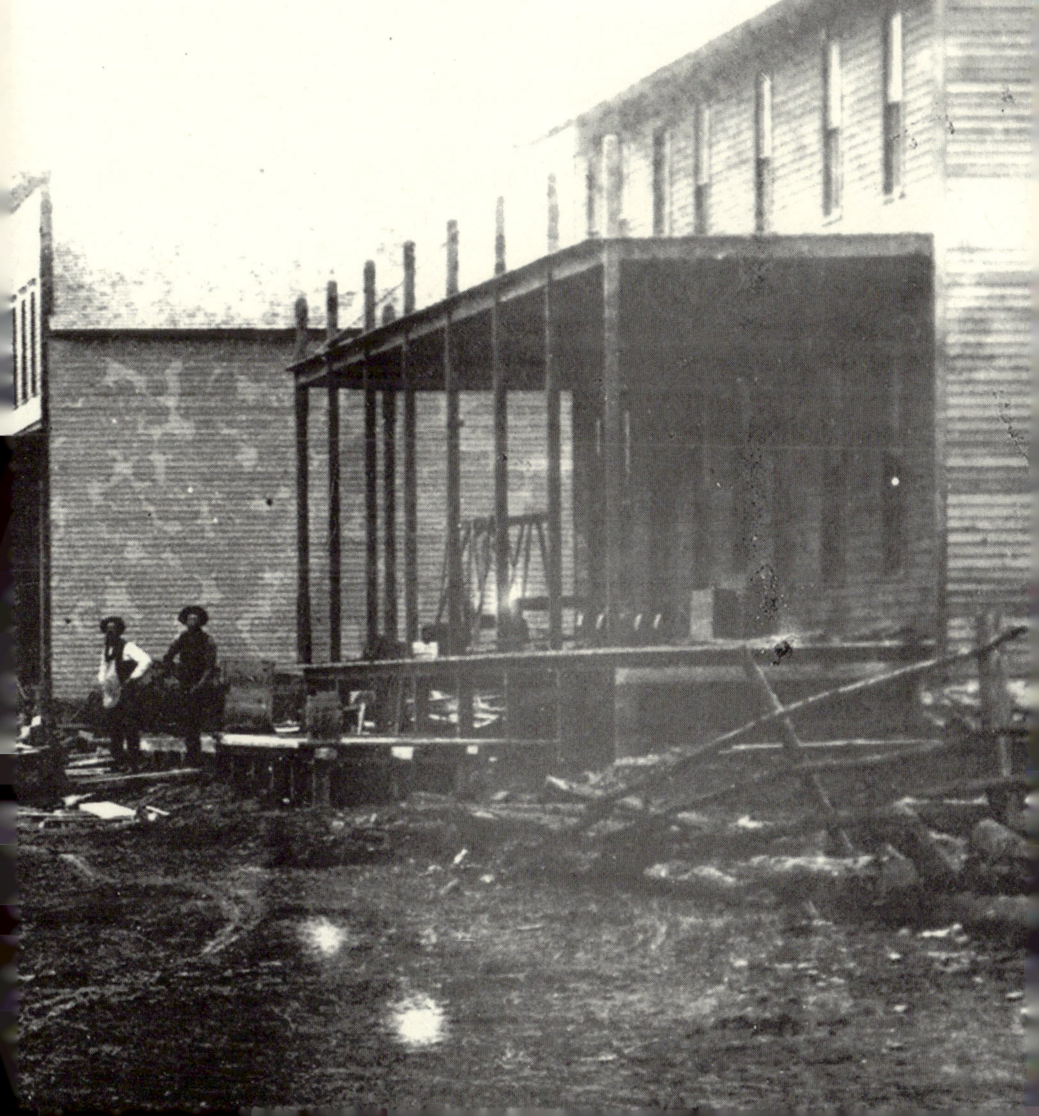

The Gold Rush is Volume 1 in the Black Hills History Tours Series

This publication is funded, in part, by the City of Deadwood and the Deadwood Historic Preservation Commission.

CIP information available upon request.

Printed in the United States of America

The paper in this book meets the guidelines for permanence and durability of the Committee on Production Guidelines for Book Longevity of the Council on Library Resources.

Please visit our website at sdhspress.com

27 26 25 24 23 1 2 3 4 5 6

Contents

The Gold Rush is Volume 1 in the Black Hills History Tours Series

Introduction
Black Hills History Tours
The Gold Rush

It all began in a Black Hills history course that I taught for Black Hills State University. Because so much of what I covered happened nearby, I decided to take my students to see the locations for themselves. These field trips allowed them to connect more directly with the past than they would in a traditional lecture-based classroom. To make the field trips even more meaningful, I developed brief outlines that explained the significance of the places we visited. Each time I taught the course, I expanded the outlines. Eventually they began to resemble full-fledged history narratives. Several students encouraged me to publish the outlines as tour guides. With their support in mind, I presented these guides to the South Dakota Historical Society Press, and they saw the value in publishing them.

While I describe the guides as resembling "full-fledged history narratives," they certainly don't resemble traditional history books. Most history texts are organized either chronologically or topically, but the tours examine history based on location. Because of this format, some topics come up repeatedly as the tour goes from one place to another, and that can be a drawback. To learn more about one topic, such as the Custer Expedition, the reader will need to find entries that are scattered throughout the guide. Fortunately, the index makes that a lot easier. There are, however, advantages to this type of organization. One is that it highlights the importance of "place" in history, and another is that it reveals the "layers of history." In other words, a succession of events often took place at each location.

Organization

The tour in your hands is the first of six tours that will hopefully be released over the next few years: this one, the Gold Rush Tour that starts in Custer; a Northern Hills Tour that starts in Lead and emphasizes locations related to the Homestake Mine; a Central Hills Tour and a Southern Hills Tour that both start in Rapid City; and a Spearfish–Deadwood–Lead Tour and a Northern Plains–Wyoming Tour that both start in Spearfish. Two of the tours are organized with a theme in mind: the Gold Rush Tour and the Homestake–Northern Hills Tour. These tours focus on locations generally related to the theme, but they also discuss historic sites encountered along the way. The other tours visit locations based on their proximity to one another. Sometimes the routes of the theme- and location-based tours overlap, and when that happens, both tours will include a discussion of the duplicated sites. This is done so that nothing of interest is missed along a tour's route. Another result of having multiple tours is that the details of some of the Black Hills' most famous landmarks are discussed in only one tour. For instance, Mount Rushmore is briefly mentioned in the Gold Rush Tour, but its full story is in the Central Hills Tour. Finally, many Black Hills towns have excellent museums, but these are only briefly mentioned. I encourage you to explore the museums on your own.

Topics

The topics included in each guide were determined by what happened at the locations the tour visits. The Gold Rush Tour, for example, follows the general trend of the Black Hills Gold Rush from its place of origin near Custer, progressing to Deadwood before it returns to Custer. Besides the discovery of gold and the early stages of the gold rush, military expeditions, active and inactive mines, and town development are all examined. Because the tour takes in much of the Black Hills, it covers topics from all eras of Black Hills history—as do all the tours. While several ghost and existing towns are visited, Deadwood and Lead, the most important mining towns in the Black Hills, are only briefly mentioned. The mining activities at these locations are discussed, but the details about these two towns are in the Northern Black Hills and Spearfish–Deadwood–Lead Tour. The Gold Rush Tour also covers historic wagon roads, railroads, tourism, and the role of the federal government, especially during the New Deal. American Indians are mentioned several times, but only as they relate to the sites the tour visits. Overall, the Gold Rush Tour covers many people, places, and events that make up Black Hills history.

Using the Guide

The tour can be done in one day, but how long it takes depends on the user. The route is divided into sections, with each section ending at a Recommended Stop. These breaks are meant to provide an opportunity to read the narrative for that location and for what lies ahead, but they can be used as bookmarks to leave the tour and return to it later. Approximate mileages are provided for each section. The mileages were checked for accuracy, but there will undoubtedly be variation.

When traveling, the sites come and go quickly and traffic can be heavy, especially in towns. Consequently, it is recommended that the tour narrative be read in advance. At some of the busiest locations, you should stop and visit the area on foot. Those who follow the tour guide do so at their own risk. The author and the publisher, the South Dakota Historical Society Press, bear no responsibility for any accidents and mishaps.

The tours follow roadways owned and maintained by government agencies, either federal, state, county, or city. Please adhere to the public rights-of-way and be respectful of private property. Courtesy of the South Dakota Department of Transportation (SDDOT), maps of the route are provided for each section, as well as an overall map for each tour. Road construction and road closures can and will affect the tours. For instance, SDDOT anticipates closing parts of US 385 through the central Black Hills beginning in 2024. If closures are encountered, you will need to improvise. The Gold Rush Tour is accurate as written in the summer of 2023.

Gold Rush Tour

The Black Hills Gold Rush started with discoveries along French Creek in the southern Black Hills and spread north. This tour will follow that general trend, and then will return south, highlighting many places, people, towns, and historical events along the way.

Origins of the Gold Rush

In the summer of 1874, the U.S. Army dispatched Lieutenant Colonel George A. Custer to the Black Hills to find a suitable location for an army post on the western edge of the Sioux Indian Reservation (later known as the Great Sioux Reservation). Custer commanded over 1,000 soldiers, including a geologist, a topographer, and a regimental band. Sixty-three American Indian scouts assisted the troop, with Custer's aide, Bloody Knife, among them. A number of civilians also came along, such as reporters from three national newspapers, two gold prospectors (Horatio Ross and William McKay), an African American cook (Sarah "Aunt Sally" Campbell), and a photographer (William H. Illingworth). Leaving Fort Abraham Lincoln near present-day Bismarck, North Dakota, the Custer Expedition crossed the plains to the west of the Black Hills, traveled past Inyan Kara Mountain, and entered the Black Hills near what is today Buckhorn, Wyoming, on 25 July. Five days later, the troop arrived at French Creek, setting up camp on the eventual townsite of Custer. With over 1,000 people, Custer's camp covered over six blocks of the current city.

Part One The French Creek Gold Rush

Route Overview: Start in Custer at the intersection of Mt. Rushmore Road (SD 89, US 16A) and 8th Street (location of Lynn's Dakotamart). Head east on SD 89/US 16A, toward the Gordon Stockade, with a detour on America Center Road. A stop is recommended at the Gordon Stockade.

Mileage starts at Lynn's Dakotamart on the corner of Mt. Rushmore Road and 8th Street.

0.0 miles **Mt. Rushmore Road and 8th Street:** The intersection of Mt. Rushmore Road and 8th Street is within the site of Custer's camp of 30–31 July 1874. The camp covered a few blocks in nearly every direction. While camped here, the prospectors Ross and McKay dug into French Creek and reportedly found flecks of gold, but not enough to cause much excitement. In the meantime, Custer, accompanied by a small group of officers and a company of cavalry, left to ascend Black Elk Peak (then known as Harney Peak) on 31 July. The men scaled two peaks before reaching the right one, and then failed to reach the highest point of the granite outcropping. That honor would go to Valentine McGillycuddy, who reached the highest point during the 1875 Newton–Jenney Expedition. The next day, 1 August, the column moved its camp about three and a half miles to the east along French Creek, looking for better grass and easier access to water.

2.6 mi **America Center Road: Turn left (north) onto America Center Road.** This route parallels French Creek and the path the Custer Expedition took as it moved to its new camp site.

Interpretative Sign: Near the intersection of America Center Road with US 16A is an interpretative sign titled "Historic Area—1874 Black Hills Expedition." It gives a brief account of the Custer Expedition and its activities in this area.

WILLOW CREEK R
2 HOUR RD
89
HOMESTEAD DR
SUMMIT ST
N 4TH ST
N BRYDEN DR
N 7TH ST
N 6TH ST
MONTGOMERY ST
N 3RD ST
N 8TH ST
HARNEY ST
CROOK ST
WASHINGTON ST
BOOT HILL LOOP
BOOT HILL RD
SURREY
ROSSE DR
16
S 7TH ST
S 8TH ST
Start:
Lynn's Dakotamart
PINE ST
GRANITE HEIGHTS DR
Custer
GORDON ST
S 10TH ST
SHERMAN ST
WILDCAT LN
HARBACH LN
BLUE BELL LN
S 1ST ST
NEEDLES DR
PARK AVE
ROSE PL
SIDNEY PARK RD
ROCK CHIMNEY RD
HAZELRODT CUTOFF

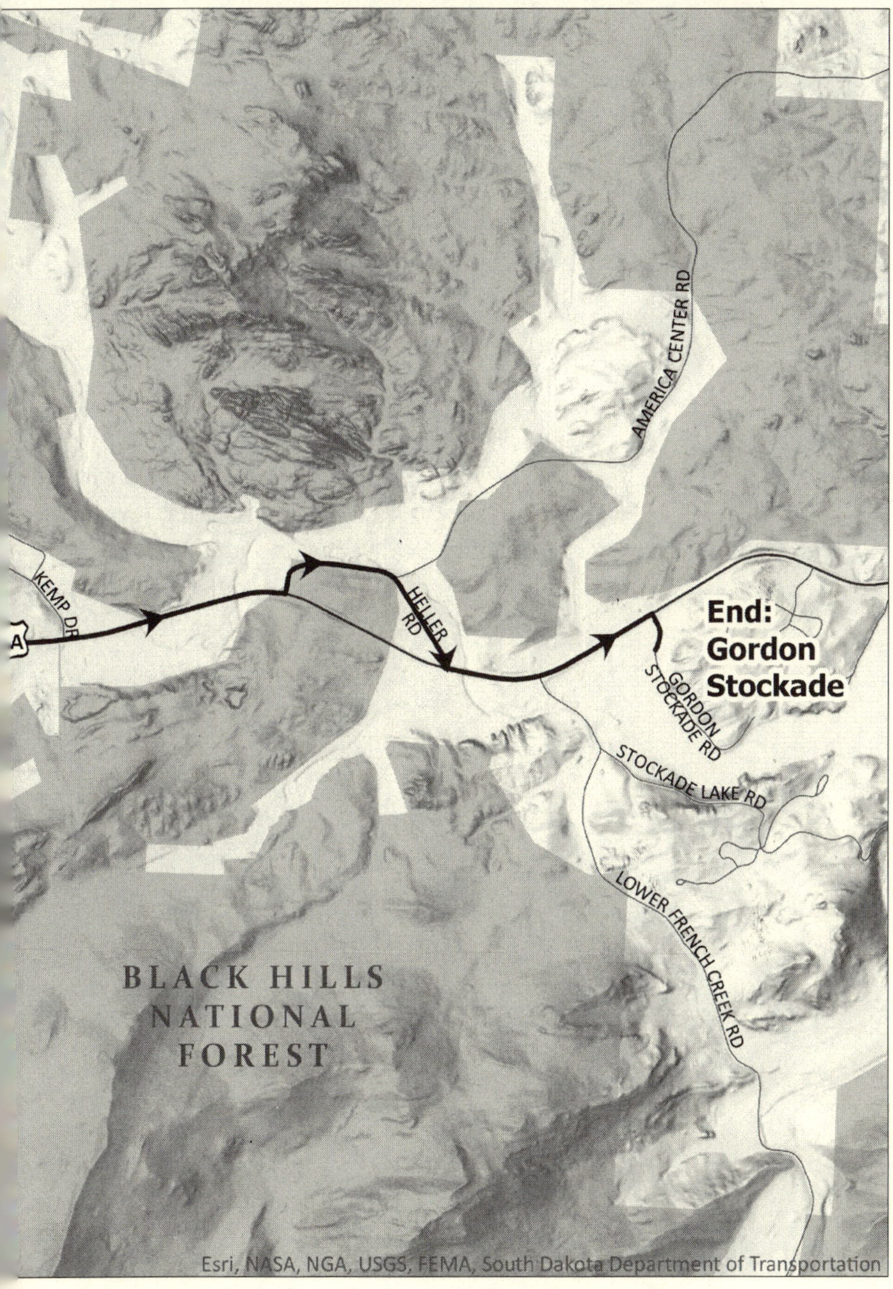
AMERICA CENTER RD
KEMP DR
HELLER RD
End: Gordon Stockade
GORDON STOCKADE RD
STOCKADE LAKE RD
LOWER FRENCH CREEK RD
BLACK HILLS NATIONAL FOREST
Esri, NASA, NGA, USGS, FEMA, South Dakota Department of Transportation

America Center Road: Black Hills businessmen and politicians, led by Paul Bellamy, gave this road its distinctive name in the mid-1940s when they promoted the nearby area as the ideal location for the United Nations' headquarters. Promotional pieces carried the logo "North America Center," and claimed it was, as the name suggested, at the geographical center of the continent. Supporters argued that the remote location would keep the UN headquarters away from political, social, economic, and military threats. Their efforts, however, gained little traction.

2.6 mi **Calamity Peak:** The granite mountain to the north of French Creek rises 1,200 feet above the valley floor. Tradition says that it was named for Martha Jane Canary, better known as Calamity Jane. In 1875, the federal government sent geologists Henry Newton and Walter P. Jenney, along with fifteen assistants and 400 soldiers under Lieutenant Colonel Richard Dodge, to map the Black Hills and to verify Custer's reports of gold. Jane accompanied the Newton–Jenney Expedition as a stowaway. While camped along French Creek, a solider supposedly

Site of the 2 August 1874 discovery of gold along French Creek, 2023. Note Calamity Peak in the background. *Author photo*

challenged Jane to climb the hill, which she promptly did. The story is probably a myth, but so is much about Jane. Although it is generally accepted that the mountain was named after Calamity Jane, the pioneer and poet John Wallace ("Captain Jack") Crawford stated that a nearby mining claim was known as Calamity Bar, and the name could have come from there.

2.8 mi **Gold Discovery Site:** Just off the road's north embankment is an interpretative sign titled "Historic Site—Gold Discovery." It was here that Custer's prospectors, Ross and McKay, discovered gold on 2 August 1874. While they had detected gold a few days earlier, they uncovered enough at this location to convince them that mining would pay handsomely. The find sent a wave of excitement through the camp, and several other people from the expedition joined them in looking for gold. Soon after, Custer dispatched a scout, Charley Reynolds, to Ft. Laramie with news of gold in the Black Hills. Newspapers quickly spread the story across the country, and the Black Hills Gold Rush was on.

2.9 mi **Heller Road Intersection: At the intersection of America Center Road and Heller Road, turn to the right (south).** The northern edge of the Custer Expedition's Permanent Camp started near this intersection and extended south along Heller Road to the other side of US 16A.

3.0 mi **Custer Expedition stone marker and John Pommer gravestone:** The two markers to the left (east) of the road mark two different military events. The Society of Black Hills Pioneers erected the stone tower to mark the 1874 Custer Expedition camp site.

The headstone marks the resting place of Private John Pommer, a German immigrant who joined the army in 1871. He came to the Black Hills with General George R. Crook's command in the fall of 1876. Crook and his men had recently fought the Miniconjou Lakotas in the Battle of Slim Buttes, north of the Black Hills, and they desperately needed supplies after the engagement. They marched to the Black Hills to restock. Already short of food, the trip challenged their endurance and became known as the Starvation or Horsemeat

March. Once in the Black Hills and resupplied, they traveled slowly to rest and recover, eventually camping along French Creek on the same ground the Custer Expedition had used two years earlier. Pommer, however, developed chronic diarrhea and died on 3 October 1876. He was originally buried a mile east of the Gordon Stockade, but with the construction of Stockade Lake his body was reinterred here.

3.2 mi **Custer Camp Marker:** To the right (west) of Heller Road is an interpretative sign that discusses the Custer Expedition and the Permanent Camp. The expedition camped in this area from 1–5 August 1874. While here, a small number of soldiers did a reconnaissance down French Creek, and Custer led a larger group on a three-day trip from 3–5 August to the Cheyenne River, about forty miles to the south. On 3 August Custer dispatched Charley Reynolds to Ft. Laramie.

3.2 mi **US 16A/Heller Road Intersection:**
Turn left (east) toward Custer State Park.

William H. Illingworth's photo of the Custer Expedition's "Permanent Camp" in French Creek Valley, August 1874. *South Dakota State Historical Society*

3.8 mi **Turn into the Gordon Stockade.**

4.0 mi **Recommended Stop at the Gordon Stockade.**

Gold Rush Interlopers: News of the Custer Expedition's discoveries attracted people from across the country who wanted their share of the riches, especially since many people were still reeling from the Panic of 1873, one of the country's worst financial crises prior to the Great Depression. Exploration and gold mining companies formed in several communities, such as Cheyenne and Bismarck, with the hope of venturing to the Black Hills. The 1868 Fort Laramie Treaty, however, forbade non-government employees from entering the Sioux Indian Reservation, which included all of present-day South Dakota west of the Missouri River. The army issued warnings to stay away and sent patrols to remove trespassers. Nevertheless, the gold seekers still came.

The Gordon Party: Two Sioux City, Iowa, promoters named Thomas Russell and Charles Collins refused to be deterred and organized an expedition. The result was the Gordon Party, named after the troop's captain, John Gordon. It comprised twenty-six men and one woman, Annie Tallent, who joined her husband, David, and their nine-year-old son, Robert. The Gordon Party left Sioux City on 6 October and successfully evaded army patrols as they traveled westward. Once in the Black Hills, they encountered Custer's trail and followed it to what was known as Custer's Gulch on French Creek, arriving on 23 December. They quickly built a square stockade, measuring eighty feet on each side, by driving thirteen-foot poles three feet into the ground. They added bastions at the corners and cut loopholes every six feet along the walls. They constructed seven cabins inside, three along each sidewall and one opposite the gate, and dug a well, uncovering small amounts of gold. They completed their work on 16 January 1875.

As the winter progressed, the ground froze, making prospecting difficult. Still, they managed to dig several holes, finding "colors" in most. Overall, life proved uneventful, with Mrs. Tallent re-reading the two books she had brought. In February, Gordon and another party member, Eph Witcher, left to recruit more gold seekers and obtain supplies. Over the next few weeks, six more bored and lonely men left for Ft. Laramie. Their meager discoveries notwithstanding, the men told exaggerated stories of gold, and the excitement spread.

The army soon found out about the interlopers and sent a patrol to remove them, but severe winter weather drove it back to Ft. Laramie. The army conscripted two of the former camp members to lead another patrol in late March 1875. With more moderate weather and knowledgeable guides, it arrived at the stockade on 5 April. The commander gave the remaining people two days to cache their tools and lay out a townsite, which they named Harney City, before they moved out. Once at Ft. Laramie, they were set free.

Visitors & Reconstructions: Since the stockade sat on French Creek, near the first discovery of gold, it became the focus of early gold seekers and a landmark for Black Hills travelers. When the government sent the Newton–Jenney Expedition in the summer of 1875, Colonel Dodge's troops camped within 400 yards of the stockade, close to, if not on, the same land as Custer's men. They called their encampment Camp Harney, and they made the stockade their supply depot. Dodge described the structure in a journal entry. In general terms, he applauded its "defensibility," but criticized it for having too few gun portals. He went on to describe the cabins as "strongly built, but very low, small and dark, and terribly filthy." Dodge's men had to clean them before storing their supplies.

Other visitors included General Crook, who made two stops at the stockade. He first came to the Black Hills with about 100 men in early July 1875 to remove miners who had illegally slipped into the region. Oddly, Crook and Dodge were working at cross purposes. Crook was attempting to uphold the 1868 Fort Laramie Treaty, while Dodge was ensuring the safety of scientists who were determining if enough value existed to violate that treaty and annex the Black Hills. As Crook prepared to leave the Black Hills with upwards of 500 trespassing miners, he and Dodge rendezvoused near the stockade on 27 July. Crook put Dodge in charge of removing miners, but Captain Edwin Pollock would soon take over that duty.

Crook, or at least his command, would again pass by the stockade over a year later, in the fall of 1876. After the Battle of Slim Buttes and

Stanley J. Morrow's photo of General George R. Crook's troops outside the Gordon Stockade, fall 1876. *South Dakota State Historical Society*

the Horsemeat March, Crook left his 2,000 troops under the command of Colonel Wesley Merritt while in the northern Black Hills. Merritt and the men then traveled through the Black Hills, stopping on French Creek to rest from late September into October, during which time Private Pommer passed away. Photographer Stanley J. Morrow took a photograph of several soldiers standing in front of the stockade. With the stockade drawing the attention of army troops and prospectors, it can perhaps be viewed as the Black Hills' first tourist attraction.

When the gold rush ended, the stockade became a forgotten relic. The moist soil of the French Creek drainage rotted the logs, and the walls quickly began to fail. It is uncertain when the stockade completely disappeared, but an 1880 newspaper story reported that three men had filed a ranch claim on the land and planned to demolish it. Six years later, in 1886, Robert Tallent lamented its loss. The stockade was certainly long gone by the 1920s, when aging Black Hills pioneers and local commercial clubs became interested in remembering people and events related to the gold rush. The Society of Black Hills Pioneers, led by Captain C. V. Gardner, believed that Annie Tallent deserved special recognition as the "First White Woman in the Black Hills," and decided to erect a monument in her honor. They were uncertain where to locate it, however. The Pioneers wanted to place it close to the stockade's location but make it accessible to travelers.

They settled for a spot just west of the stockade's site on what was known as the State Game Lodge Highway. That made the monument visible from French Creek, but it also guaranteed plenty of visitors. At that time, the road was a main entry into Custer State Park. The monument's dedication in late August 1924 drew a large crowd and a variety of notable South Dakota personages, including U.S. senator Peter Norbeck and South Dakota poet laureate Badger Clark. Black Hills residents celebrated Tallent as a true pioneer. After she returned to the region, she became well-known as a teacher, eventually becoming superintendent of public instruction in Rapid City, and wrote a Black Hills history book titled *The Black Hills, or, The Last Hunting Ground of the Dakotahs*. In more recent years she has been vilified, with her name removed from a Rapid City elementary school, partly because of insensitive comments about American Indians in her book. Highway realignment later bypassed her monument. The former State Game Lodge Highway is now known as Lower French Creek/Stockade Lake Road.

As the Tallent monument went up, a group of Custer residents led by C. C. O'Harra, president of the South Dakota School of Mines, sought to identify the stockade's exact location. In July 1924, the O'Harra party successfully located log stumps from the fort's upright posts. They dug up a few, putting one on display at the School of Mines' museum, and sent another to a Gordon Party descendant. Their discovery set in motion an effort to rebuild the stockade. Captain Gardner of the Pioneers again led the way by collecting donations, while the Custer Commercial Club promoted the project. Their efforts brought quick results, and the rebuilt stockade was dedicated on 20 August 1925. Sadly, the structure quickly fell into disrepair. Two problems existed. One was that the reconstructed stockade was made of log slabs instead of whole logs, hurting the building's integrity, and the other was that livestock, allowed to graze next to it, pushed over the log slabs.

As the rebuilt stockade failed, public money became available during the New Deal. The state took control of the structure in 1933 and looked to rebuild it using Civilian Conservation Corps labor (the CCC, a key part of President Franklin D. Roosevelt's New Deal, provided manual labor jobs to millions of young men between 1933 and

1942). The project, however, was delayed while Stockade Lake took priority. Finally, with the support of the Custer State Park board of directors, the state historian (who verified the structure's layout), and the CCC, a new structure was built in 1941. Some people say that the rising water of Stockade Lake required moving the structure 200 yards to the north, but not everyone agrees that it was moved. In any case, the CCC built a more accurate version, using whole logs set into the ground. The rebuilt stockade became a minor tourist attraction, but it suffered the same fate as prior versions: the logs rotted. By 1970, wires held the structure together. The state came to see the old fort as a safety hazard and discussed destroying it in 2000. Local protests persuaded the state to build a new version instead. The rebuilt stockade opened in 2005 at a cost of $825,000 of state and federal money. This time the builders treated the logs with a preservative and set them on concrete foundations instead of sinking them into the soil. Four of the cabins were also reconstructed. The state restored three cabins from an earlier version.

Part Two Custer City

The First City of the Gold Rush

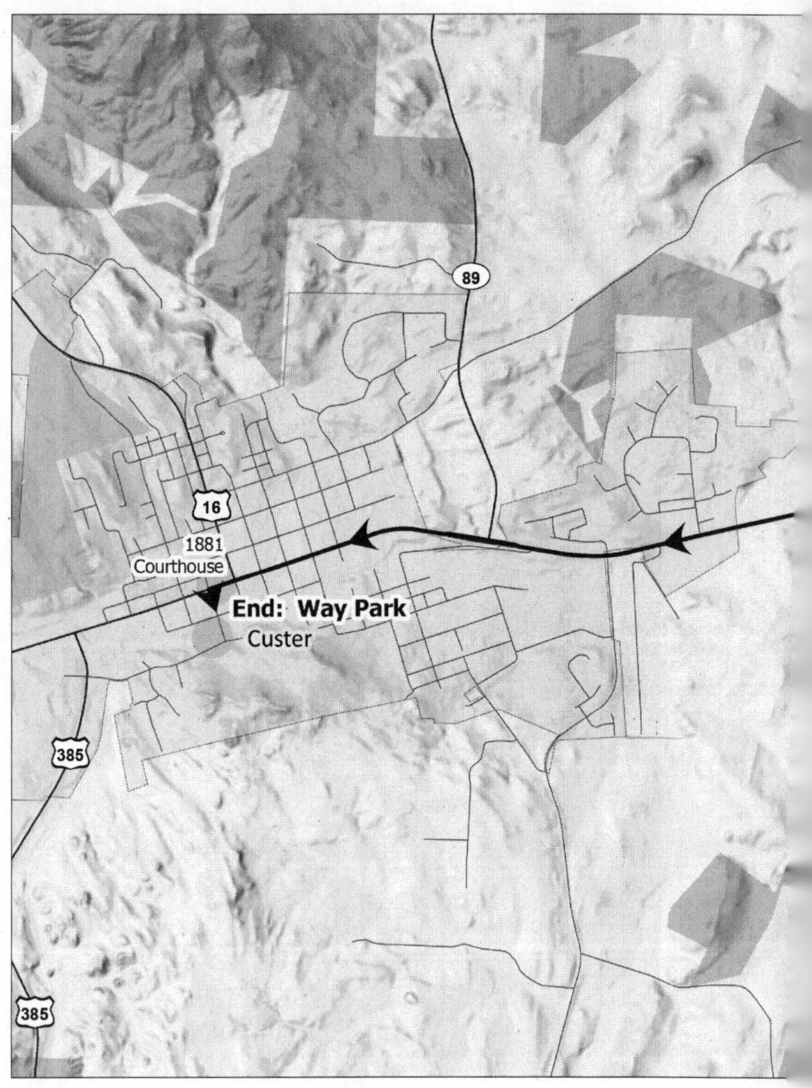

Route Overview: From the Gordon Stockade, turn left (west) and take US 16A to downtown Custer. Recommended Stop at Way Park, the courtyard of the County Courthouse, opposite the 1881 Courthouse.

Mileage starts at Gordon Stockade.

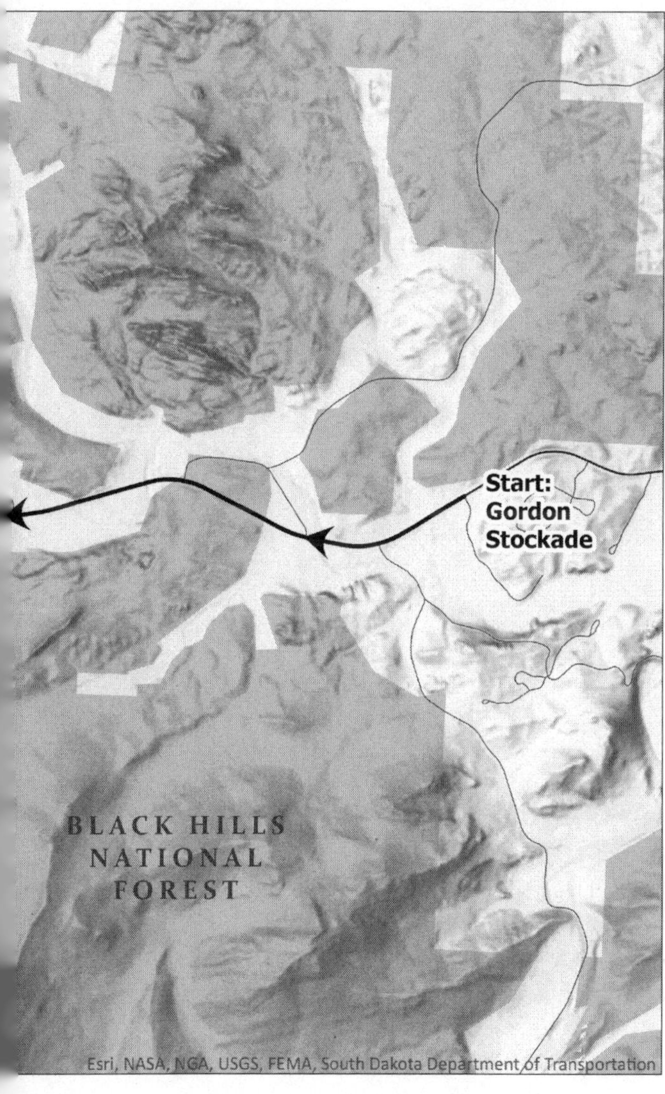

0.0 mi **Gordon Stockade Parking Lot: Return to US 16A.**

0.1 mi **Junction with US 16A: Turn left (west).**

0.4 mi **Lower French Creek Road, Custer County Road 341:** This road was once known as State Game Lodge Highway and served as one of the entrances into Custer State Park. US 16A, built to the north of Stockade Lake, replaced it.

Annie Tallent Monument: The monument to Gordon Party member Annie Tallent sits 0.2 miles down Lower French Creek Road. The Society of Black Hills Pioneers erected it in 1924 to honor the person they described as the "First White Woman in the Black Hills."

The Annie Tallent Monument, with the reconstructed Gordon Stockade in the background, 2022. *Author photo*

2.7 mi **Sidney Park Road:** On the left is Sidney Park Road, named after the Sidney-to-Custer Trail. From Sidney, Nebraska, the trail passed through Camp (later Fort) Robinson and entered the Black Hills through Buffalo Gap, along Beaver Creek. After swinging around Point of Rocks, a large outcropping near Pringle, the trail ran north, first paralleling today's US 385 and then Sidney Park Road into Custer. This route was heavily traveled during the early days of the gold rush, but when Deadwood became the focus of the excitement, most of the Sidney traffic bypassed the Buffalo Gap–Beaver Creek route and went up the east side of the Black Hills, going through Rapid City, Crook City, and on to Deadwood.

3.0 mi **SD 89, Sylvan Lake Road:** The road on the right (south) leads to Sylvan Lake and Sylvan Lake Lodge.

3.6 mi **Custer YMCA:** Two blocks south of the intersection of US 16A (Mt. Rushmore Road) and 7th Street, and barely visible from the road, is a large log structure at 644 Crook Street. The Custer Women's Civic Club saw a need for a recreation and community center and spearheaded the construction of this building. The group hired Berge Berglund, a Norwegian log worker, to build the fifty-by-one-hundred-foot structure and persuaded First Lady Grace Coolidge to dedicate it in 1927 while she and the president were vacationing in Custer State Park. Known as the Custer Community Center or the Grace Coolidge Memorial Log Building, today it houses Custer's YMCA.

Custer's First Jail: A small stone structure labeled Custer's First Jail sits in front of the Community Center. An informational sign states that it originally sat across the street and that its first occupant was Wilber Todd, the person who built it. He apparently spent his pay on alcohol, got drunk, and was arrested.

Custer's first jail, with the Grace Coolidge Memorial Building in the background, 2022. *Author photo*

3.8 mi **Custer Business District:** The blocks that run from 7th to 4th Streets on US 16A (Mt. Rushmore Road) are the center of Custer's business district. While primarily targeted at the tourist trade, there are several structures that highlight Custer's history.

Kleemann House (1883), 619 Mt. Rushmore Road: Paul Kleemann built the prominent two-story brick structure on the righthand (north) side of the street. A native of Germany, Kleemann came to the Black Hills in 1877. He tried mining at Hayward and Rockerville before arriving in Custer in 1880. Although he continued to dabble in mining, he entered the hotel business and built this namesake property in 1883. The main floor had five rooms, including a bar and a dining room, and the upstairs was divided into nine bedrooms. Kleemann promoted it as the "only first-class hotel in town," and he apparently entertained such guests as Buffalo Bill Cody. Kleemann operated the hotel until his death in 1902. Family members took control and eventually sold it. A succession of owners gave the facility a variety of names, including Pine Cone Inn and General Custer Motor Lodge. The old building fell into disrepair by the late twentieth century, and the city condemned it in 1991. New owners came to the rescue in 2010, elegantly restoring and remodeling it into an upscale vacation rental that opened in 2012.

With the hotel's restoration, Kleemann's legacy lives on in Custer. At the time of his death, he was praised for his work on behalf of the city and county, but he was also described as blunt and outspoken, earning him both friends and enemies. The *Custer Chronicle* described him as "rough at times" but with a kind and generous heart.

First National Bank of Dakota Territory (1911), 588 Mt. Rushmore Road: On the southwest corner of the intersection of Mt. Rushmore Road and 6th Street is a sandstone commercial structure built for the First National Bank in 1911. The bank opened in 1881 and moved into a wood frame building on this corner in 1883. This building replaced it. Its heavy stonework and rectangular windows resemble several sandstone structures built in the Black Hills in the late nineteenth and early twentieth centuries.

“The Heidepriem Co.” (1910), 538 Mt. Rushmore Road: In 1910 Fred Heidepriem built the large two-story brick building with “The Heidepriem Co.” painted across its top. Heidepriem, a Black Hills pioneer, walked from Cheyenne to Custer in August 1876. He searched for gold in the area around Sunday Gulch, near today’s Sylvan Lake, finding four nuggets but little else. He joined the rush to Deadwood Gulch, but with the diggings already overcrowded, he worked as a carpenter and cabinetmaker instead and reportedly built the first frame dwelling in Lead City. Looking for a stable income, he returned to Custer and went into the construction and furniture business. He built Custer’s first schoolhouse and then opened a small store in 1879. There he made all types of furniture, including caskets, and he soon became an undertaker.

As business grew, Heidepriem had this commercial structure built. While he focused on woodworking and undertaking, his wife and children ran the store. By the time of his death in 1917, Heidepriem’s two sons, Fred and Eric, had taken over the business. They continued to run Heidepriem Furniture until 1959. When they closed, local newspapers called it the oldest family-operated business in the Black Hills. While running the store, the Heidepriem family also became community leaders; one son served in the state legislature, and a daughter wrote the script for the Gold Discovery Days pageant. Custer residents performed the pageant annually as part of a community celebration in the early twentieth century.

Garlock Building (1890), 522 Mt. Rushmore Road: The Garlock Building is just down the block from the Heidepriem building. Thomas (“T. V.”) Van Garlock arrived in Custer in 1884 and joined A. T. Van Devort in the hardware, machinery, and mine supply business. Garlock took sole ownership of the enterprise in 1886 and built this brick Commercial style structure in 1890. Its decorative cornices, arched upstairs windows, and attractive facade led the Custer newspaper to describe the Italianate-designed building as the most elegant ever erected in Custer. Garlock changed his business over the years. He started with a hardware store, then converted it to a general mercantile, and finally opened an automobile agency. He became interested in cars early on, and when he purchased a single-seat model in 1901, he was credited with having the first automobile in the Black Hills, if not the state. Garlock also became involved in banking and city government. To provide a place for meetings and entertainment he built an opera house in 1894. By the time of his death in 1920, he was described as one of the best known and well-liked Custer County residents. The Garlock Building has housed a variety of businesses since Garlock's passing, including a saloon. Today it is home to the *Custer Chronicle*.

"Oldest Saloon in the Black Hills," 508 Mt. Rushmore Road: In front of the Gold Pan Saloon on the south side of the street is a sign that says it is the "Oldest Saloon in the Black Hills." Such claims are hard to verify, but since Custer was the first town established during the gold rush, it could be true.

"Historic Site," 541 Mt. Rushmore Road: Over the door of Baker's Bakery & Cafe, the bright pink building on the north side of the street, is a sign that says, "Historic Site." It goes on to state, "Site of Saloon Where James Fowler (Alias Fly Speck Billy) Murdered Abe Barnes in February 1881. Billy was hanged by a mob." The event mentioned on the sign did occur in Custer and is discussed at an upcoming stop. It is difficult, however, to determine if this is the actual location. Not many years ago, Custer entrepreneurs featured this affair in a small show and tourist business known as Fly Speck Billy Trading Post. A dummy was suspended by a hangman's rope from the trading post's sign. This location once housed a bar and could have been where Billy killed Barnes. But it may also have been chosen randomly.

3.9 mi **Intersection of US 16A (Mt. Rushmore Road) and US 385 at stoplight: Continue west for one block.**

4.0 mi **1881 Courthouse, 411 Mt. Rushmore Road:** The two-story sandstone courthouse was constructed soon after Custer became the county seat in 1881. The tall windows, decorative brickwork, and prominent cornice reflect its Italianate design. Several Black Hills buildings built between 1880 and 1910 have similar features. Two wings that were added in 1915 have the same basic design, but with less ornamentation. The county constructed a new courthouse in the 1970s, and this city landmark was converted into a museum.

Courthouse encounter: The old courthouse was the scene of the infamous Custer Courthouse Riot in 1973. The trouble began in January of that year when Darld Schmitz, a white man, wounded Wesley Bad Heart Bull, a Lakota, in what was described as a violent barroom brawl in Buffalo Gap. Bad Heart Bull died en route to the hospital. Schmitz was arrested and charged with manslaughter. Outraged at what they believed was a lenient charge, around 200 American Indians, including several American Indian Movement (AIM) members, planned to protest during the preliminary hearing. As the authorities prevented AIM supporters from entering the courthouse, a police officer knocked down the dead man's mother and a riot erupted. Around twenty people gained entrance to the building, but others wrecked police cruisers and set fire to cars, the chamber of commerce building, two gas stations, and the courthouse. The police arrested thirty people. The riot changed little, and Schmitz was later convicted of manslaughter. Bad Heart Bull's death, along with the earlier killing of Raymond Yellow Thunder in Gordon, Nebraska, are often cited as catalysts for the occupation of Wounded Knee.

Wounded Knee II: Later that month, around 250 American Indians occupied the hamlet of Wounded Knee, site of the 1890 massacre, to protest a variety of injustices. The immediate cause was a political dispute between traditionalists and the reservation government led by Pine Ridge tribal chairman Dick Wilson, who had recently evaded impeachment on numerous charges including corruption and nepotism. A seventy-one-day armed standoff began on 27 February 1973, when U.S. Marshals, FBI agents, and Bureau of Indian Affairs (BIA) representatives blocked roads and besieged the occupiers. Two of the occupiers were killed; fourteen more were wounded, as well as one U.S. Marshal. The standoff ended on 8 May when the Nixon administration agreed to discuss treaty rights, but the talks brought little change. Wounded Knee has been a controversial topic ever since, especially as it gained international attention and left many Lakotas divided between supporting AIM and resenting its presence on the reservation.

4.0 mi **Recommended Stop in Downtown Custer:**
Way Park, 424 Mt. Rushmore Road, the courtyard of the County Courthouse, opposite the 1881 Courthouse.
Way Park: This park is named for Henry Way. A noted Custer citizen and county judge, Way donated the park and cabin to the city.

The Flick Cabin: The City of Custer's website gives this narrative about the log cabin: "The Dr. Flick cabin was the first building erected in the Black Hills. Dr. D. W. Flick built it of substantial hand-hewn logs and designed it as a home for his family." It is difficult to verify this account. Dr. Daniel Flick arrived early in the gold rush, and several sources credit him with building one of the first cabins in Custer. But it is unknown if it was the first cabin in the Black Hills, which seems unlikely. Henry Way identified this log building as Custer's first cabin in 1923, nearly fifty years after the gold rush. Way also placed the Shankland family in the cabin, not Dr. Flick. The structure does date from Custer's early days, although it is not in its original location. Way had it moved from where it once stood, where the gold discovery monument now stands.

Despite the uncertain early history, an apocryphal story has been told about the cabin. It states that Flick started building the cabin in August 1875, but he left it unfinished when General Crook removed him and the other trespassing miners. Captain Pollock supposedly finished the cabin and used it as his headquarters when he took over guarding the Black Hills. After he departed, Captain Jack Crawford took up residence there. When Flick returned in April 1876, he insisted the cabin was his and threw Crawford's belongings into the street. The two men took their dispute to a miners' court, where the jury ruled in Flick's favor. He used it as a residence and an office until he left for Rapid City around 1880. The Flick–Crawford dispute may well have happened, but no evidence of it can be found in the historical records.

The Flick Cabin and Gold Discovery Monument in Custer, 2022. *Author photo*

Horatio Ross Memorial & Gold Discovery Monument: The stone tower with the gold pan on top was meant to recognize the first discovery of gold and the person who discovered it, but two things stand out. First, Horatio Ross and William McKay, members of the Custer Expedition, are generally credited as the discoverers of gold, but the memorial credits only Ross, probably because he lived in Custer until his 1904 death at the age of sixty-six and is buried in the Custer cemetery. The second issue is the listed discovery date of 27 July. When Ross was called upon to relate the story of discovery, he may have used that date, but the expedition was camped on Castle Creek, near a stream called Gold Run Creek, on 27 July. There is a report that McKay uncovered small amounts of gold there, but no other evidence exists. It is much more widely accepted that the first significant gold discovery happened on French Creek, close to Custer's Permanent Camp, on 2 August. These discrepancies aside, the monument's tower highlights a variety of local rocks and minerals, including rose quartz and petrified wood.

The Monument's Creation and Gold Discovery Days: By the early 1920s, Black Hills pioneers and area commercial clubs had become interested in highlighting the region's past. Whereas the pioneers wanted to celebrate their generation's achievements, the commercial clubs saw an opportunity to promote tourism. No matter the motivation, the Custer Business Men's Club led the charge in building the Ross gold discovery monument in 1921. The group collected money and hired stonemason Monte Nystrom to erect the stone tower out of donated rock specimens. They set the dedication for 27 July, mistakenly believing that was the anniversary of Ross's gold discovery, and they also erred in claiming that Ross had made that discovery only a few blocks from the monument's site. Regardless, the dedication was part of a "Pioneer Day" celebration that included a parade, a barbecue, a baseball game, speeches, band music, and other festivities. With thousands of people from throughout the Black Hills attending, the occasion's success inspired the Custer Women's Civic Club to start the Gold Discovery Days Pageant in 1922, a four-part event with performances depicting the "creation of the universe," "Lakota culture," "discovery of gold," and "growth of Custer City." The pageant soon morphed into a three-day rodeo, but it was discontinued in the 1950s. It has recently been resurrected as a summer celebration with a carnival, a car show, an arts & crafts fair, volleyball, a 5k run, hot-air balloon rides, and a parade.

Custer City's founding: Custer City got its start when General Crook was removing miners from the Black Hills in 1875. With Crook's approval, miners met on 10 August, just before their forced departure, to found Custer City. They formed a town-site company, laid out the town, divided it into lots, and ran a lottery to distribute them. Custer City replaced a town called Stonewall City that had been laid out a month earlier. A few miners began building cabins in Custer City, but development came to an abrupt halt as most left with Crook. The general allowed a few men to stay behind to guard the tools and belongings that the departing prospectors left at the site.

Army removal and boom: When Captain Pollock assumed responsibility for removing the miners, he took a harsher stand than Crook. After establishing his headquarters in Custer, he and his troops searched the Black Hills for trespassers. He confined the captured men to an outdoor jail called a "bull-pen" that sat just west of Way Park. He then sent them under guard to Ft. Laramie. By fall 1875, the army had worked to uphold the 1868 Fort Laramie Treaty for almost a year, but President Ulysses S. Grant was under political pressure to open the Black Hills to miners and settlers. Recognizing the futility of keeping the prospectors out, Grant gave up and ordered the troops withdrawn in late 1875. Gold seekers rushed in as Pollock and his troops left, bringing Custer to life. One entrepreneur brought a steam-powered sawmill, and nearly 100 rough-cut houses and a small number of businesses soon appeared. A Cheyenne newspaper described Custer City as a "lively" place with 500 or 600 people by February 1876, and it quickly grew to a population of a few thousand. Custer was the Black Hills' first town.

Sidney and Cheyenne Trails: The two most important trails to the Black Hills, the Sidney Trail from the east and the Cheyenne Trail from the west, converged in Custer. The Cheyenne Trail entered the Black Hills through Red Canyon, which starts just north of Edgemont, and followed Pleasant Valley to a location about four miles west of Custer, now called Fourmile. The trail then turned toward town. The town's status as a crossroads meant that most gold seekers, no matter their ultimate destination, came to Custer in the early days of the rush and helped it boom. To handle the wagon traffic, the town founders created a wide Main Street to allow bull teams to turn in the road. Unlike most mining towns, Custer's valley location offered plenty of room. Once in town, prospectors who wished to head north could choose from a couple of trails. One left town close to today's US 385, and another went up French Creek.

Violence in Custer: Custer experienced all the problems of a gold rush boomtown, which naturally included violence. Clashes with American Indians were very pronounced in the camp's early days. The camp was readily accessible from the neighboring plains, allowing gold seekers and their Lakota pursuers to enter easily. The warriors wanted to keep the interlopers out, but also to take their horses. One observer estimated that Lakota warriors killed twelve whites on the outskirts of town or on nearby roads in one month in 1876. The ongoing threat spurred Custer's residents to form militia units. Captain Jack Crawford led one group of 125 men known as the Custer Minutemen, but they proved ineffective at deterring violence. Within the camp itself, residents sometimes turned to guns to settle their differences. Ironically, the first killing was an accident: In late February 1876 two partners got drunk and started taking turns shooting at a bucket. One was killed by an errant bullet. A miners' court quickly tried the perpetrator. Since the shooting was accidental, the jury found him innocent of murder, but guilty of shooting firearms in town, which resulted in a thirty-dollar fine.

This killing was followed by what one chronicler called the "first authenticated" Black Hills murder. In March 1876, C. C. Clayton, described as an "all-around desperado," shot a one-time mail carrier named Boueyer, claiming he had stolen his horses. A miners' court found Clayton guilty and wanted him hanged. The judge instead recognized that the court had no legal standing and ordered him banished from camp. As the prospectors moved on and the population plunged, the chances for gunplay quickly diminished. Gold camps, no matter their size, still had moments of violence, and Custer was no exception. In 1881, James Fowler, known as Fly Speck Billy, invited Abe Barnes to have a drink with him. When Barnes refused, the drunken Billy shot and killed him. The sheriff arrested Billy, but a local vigilante committee intervened and hanged him. A Deadwood paper put it more delicately when it said Billy died from a "sudden pressure to his windpipe."

From Boom to Bust: Custer's boom proved brief. The gold was sparse and difficult to recover. Part of the problem came from French Creek's limited water and lazy flow. Miners liked substantial water and a good current to operate their sluice boxes. They also found few quartz outcroppings that carried gold. Many soon left, either for home or for new diggings in the north, especially when stories of great finds in Deadwood Gulch filtered through the Black Hills in the spring of 1876. Custer City was all but deserted. One observer counted only fourteen residents remaining. The trails still came through, however, providing opportunities to sell supplies, and the grassy valleys encouraged small cattle ranches to open. More importantly, some miners found only frustration in Deadwood and returned to rework old claims for previously overlooked gold ore outcroppings—a pattern that repeated itself throughout the Black Hills. By 1880, Custer's population had stabilized around 300.

Developments in the 1880s helped guarantee Custer's permanence. The residents successfully persuaded Custer County voters to move the county seat from Hayward to Custer, leading to the construction of the impressive 1881 courthouse. The discovery of tin ore northeast of Black Elk Peak in 1883 brought further growth, especially as English investors took charge of what was called the Harney Peak Tin Company, buying hundreds of claims and creating a new boom. The arrival of the Burlington & Missouri River Railroad in 1890 seemingly guaranteed economic security. The rail connection allowed for mica mines to open, commercial timber harvests to expand, and tourism to begin, at least in small ways, causing the town's population to more than double.

Pegmatite Mines: After the initial rush to Custer had ended, gold played only a minor role in the town's future. Instead of gold, miners sought minerals known as pegmatites, crystals that contain industrial or rare earth minerals such as mica, feldspar, and spodumene (lithium). Chemically identical to the host granite, pegmatite crystals form when a portion of the igneous fluids cool more slowly than the neighboring rock. Feldspar has been used in fire retardants, caulks, sealants, glass, ceramic tile, glazes, and bricks; mica in oil and water drilling, sound dampening, insulation, and paints; and spodumene in lubricants and medicine. In the Black Hills, pegmatites are generally found around Black Elk Peak, near Custer, and in the northwestern Black Hills near the Wyoming border. The pegmatite mines in the Custer area have most frequently produced mica and feldspar. To the west of town are two of the more famous pegmatite mines because of the minerals found there: the Tin Mountain Mine and the Tip Top Mine. Black Hills mineralogist Tom Loomis writes that 250 mineral species are found in the Black Hills, twenty-two of them new to science, and the Tip Top Mine accounts for the majority of these.

Much like gold mining, pegmatite mines had periods of boom and bust. Successful pegmatite mining depended on demand and price, which varied widely over the years. For instance, the early electrical industry used mica for its insulating qualities, causing several mines to open, but other products replaced it in the early twentieth century. When cassiterite, a type of tin ore, was identified, it caused a frenzy of speculation, bringing significant development to Keystone and Hill City between 1883 and 1893. In the end, the extent and value of the tin ore was limited. Feldspar was the most important pegmatite in the 1920s and 1930s, with a number of mines and processing plants opening. It is still mined today. Most pegmatite operations were modest, with miners digging small open pit and underground workings to access the minerals. Reminders of these activities still exist, from abandoned mines to names of roads.

Pacer Corp.: The Pacer Corporation operated a feldspar plant just west of Custer until its recent closing. Consolidated Feldspar built the original mill in the 1920s. After it burned in 1958, International Minerals rebuilt it, and Pacer Corp. acquired it in 1972. Established in 1970, Pacer Corp. also mined and processed mica. After a 2018 change in ownership, the company bought more mines, including the Etta and the Tin Mountain, and updated its processes, but it seems that was insufficient for the company to survive.

Custer Today: The county and federal governments are important year-round employers in Custer. The U.S. Forest Service has its Black Hills headquarters here. Summer tourism also adds a big boost to the economy, with Custer State Park, Wind Cave, Jewel Cave, and Crazy Horse Memorial nearby. The streets of Custer are filled with visitors in the summer but are quiet in the winter.

Bear Rock: As a final note about the Custer gold rush: 1.3 miles west of Way Park is Bear Rock. Prospectors used this natural landmark on French Creek to orient the Cheyenne Mining District, the region's first gold district. On 11 June 1875, miners met at Bear Rock and made it their "location monument." In other words, it became the starting point for staking and numbering mining claims. They also appointed a claim recorder, who had an office either in a nearby cabin or in a cave. Early photos show a cabin in front of the rock, which may have

Stanley J. Morrow's photograph of Bear Rock, west of Custer, ca. fall 1876. *South Dakota State Historical Society*

been the recorder's office. One report says it was the first cabin in the Black Hills, other than those in the Gordon Stockade, which was built in March 1875. This may or may not be true. It was torn down in 1880. Bear Rock is not on the tour route and it is a little difficult to find. A house and a car port partially obscure it. The Society of Black Hills Pioneers placed a marker near the rock in the 1920s.

Part Three **Hill City**
The Second City of the Gold Rush

Route Overview: From Way Park travel one block east to the intersection with the stoplight. Turn left (north) on US 16/385 and travel to Hill City. Once at Hill City, take the bypass and turn into the Mickelson Trailhead in Tracy Park for a Recommended Stop.

Mileage starts from Way Park.

0.0 mi **Way Park: Turn right (east) onto Mt. Rushmore Road, US 16/385.**

0.1 mi **Intersection at Stoplight: Turn left (north) on US 16/385.**
Custer Expedition: Custer and his column of over 1,000 people entered and left French Creek Valley on a trail that sits near US 385. The expedition came into the valley from the west, intersecting with US 385's eventual route just outside of town. Leaving town, Custer followed the same path before angling to the west farther up the hill, about where Medicine Mountain Road connects with US 385. In both directions, the expedition would have had a good view of Thunderhead Mountain, which is now Crazy Horse Memorial.

1.0 mi **U.S. Forest Service's Black Hills Headquarters:** In 1897 President Grover Cleveland used his executive authority under the Forest Reserve Act of 1891 to create the Black Hills Forest Reserve. Local outcry motivated South Dakota's congressional delegation to challenge the designation. Their efforts, however, only delayed it one year. In 1905, President Theodore Roosevelt transferred the nation's forest reserves from the Department of the Interior to the Department of Agriculture, and they became National Forests. The original Black Hills National Forest encompassed much of what is in the forest today, but it has gone through several administrative changes. President William H. Taft divided the forest into two units in 1910. The northern section took the Black Hills National Forest name and was

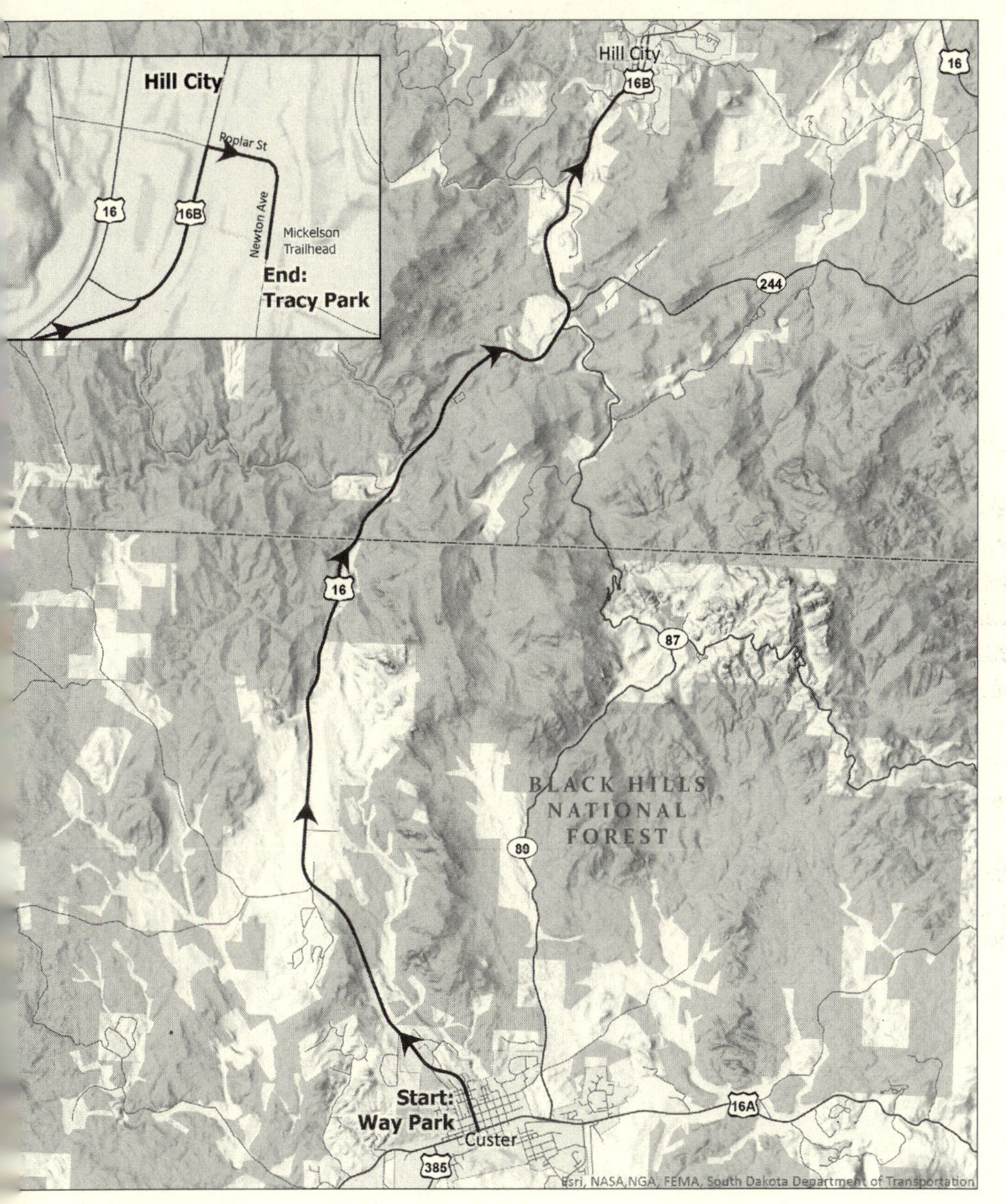
Hill City
Poplar St
16
16B
Newton Ave
Mickelson
Trailhead
End:
Tracy Park
Hill City
16B
16
244
16
87
BLACK HILLS
NATIONAL
FOREST
89
Start:
Way Park
Custer
16A
385
Esri, NASA, NGA, FEMA, South Dakota Department of Transportation

headquartered in Deadwood. The southern section became Harney National Forest, with its office in Custer. While the change was made for more effective management, in 1954 President Dwight D. Eisenhower recombined the forests in the name of better efficiency, with Custer chosen as the headquarters. This office complex was built in 1971–1972.

4.5 mi **Crazy Horse Memorial:** The inspiration for this carving began with Oglala Lakota chief Henry Standing Bear, a maternal cousin of Crazy Horse. Partly motivated by the work on Mount Rushmore, he saw a mountain carving as a way to preserve his people's culture and history. After visiting with various sculptors, including Rushmore's Gutzon Borglum, Standing Bear turned to Korczak Ziolkowski, who had worked for Borglum during the summer of 1939. A self-taught and relatively inexperienced sculptor from New England, Ziolkowski gained fame by winning a first-place medal at the 1939 New York World's Fair. Standing Bear told Ziolkowski that a sculpture would bring hope and reconciliation to his people, and that it should be in the Black Hills, a place sacred to the Lakotas. Ziolkowski agreed to come to the Black Hills in 1947 and soon after accepted the challenge. He and Standing Bear selected Thunderhead Mountain, with Ziolkowski gaining control of it by staking mining claims. He made drawings and models of the proposed carving and dedicated the project in 1948. For the next thirty-four years, Ziolkowski made slow progress on the memorial. With his family's help, he also developed a visitor center, a museum, a business, and a home, and dreamed of building a university and a medical school. When he died in 1982, he was laid to rest in a tomb at the base of the memorial. Today the complex includes the Indian Museum of North America, the Native American Educational and Cultural Center, and the Indian University of North America.

Ruth Ziolkowski: When Ziolkowski came to the Black Hills he was married to Dorothy Comstock. She came from a prominent New England family, and the couple had a daughter, Ann. Not long after arriving in the Black Hills, they divorced. She claimed mental cruelty. In 1950 Ziolkowski married Ruth Ross, a student from New

England who had followed him west to volunteer at the memorial in 1947. They had ten children together, five boys and five girls. Ruth handled many of the day-to-day operations, from running a timber mill, a dairy farm, and a gift shop, to overseeing improvements. She took over the Crazy Horse Memorial project upon Korczak's death. Ruth passed away in 2014. Some of the children and several grandchildren remain involved. After Ruth passed away, the Crazy Horse Foundation Board appointed Laurie Becvar as the memorial's CEO. The choice surprised some, as she came from outside the family and organization. After several years at the helm, Becvar left the memorial project. Whitney Rencountre II was selected as CEO in 2022.

Odds and ends: The people at the Crazy Horse Memorial take pride in the fact that they have never accepted federal aid, partly because they do not want federal oversight. There are some ironies with the project. First, no known image of Crazy Horse exists. The design was Ziolkowski's best guess. Second, some Lakotas see dynamiting the mountain as violating the Black Hills' sacredness.

Mickelson Trail: This hiking and biking trail is visible just east of US 385 immediately after the turn into Crazy Horse Memorial. The trail sits on the Burlington Railroad bed that was built in 1890. The Burlington used the line until 1983. Soon after its abandonment, South Dakota Game, Fish, and Parks officials began discussing turning the railroad right-of-way into a trail. The idea sat dormant until the Burlington began pulling up track and dismantling trestles in 1985. Recognizing that the cost of replacing trestles might end any chance of developing a trail, Guy Edwards, a Rapid City businessman, began organizing a grassroots effort to save the trestles and create a trail. Helping his cause was the 1983 National Trails System Act. The federal government passed this law to slow what seemed to be a dramatic loss of rail lines during the 1980s. It stated that inactive roadbeds could be preserved in a "railbank," with the hope that they would be returned to rail use in the future. In the interim, the roadbed could be used as a trail. Edwards also gained support from National Rails to Trails, a private organization that originated in the 1960s. By the time Edwards began promoting a Black Hills trail, the national group had successfully converted 21,000 miles of former railroad roadbeds into trails.

Edwards organized a local rails-to-trails committee and quickly sought an agency that would take control of the roadbed and develop a trail. He ran into several roadblocks. Prior to the railbank law, abandoned railroad rights-of-way traditionally reverted to neighboring property owners, and while most of the rail line ran through National Forest land, the handful of private landowners along the route filed a lawsuit attempting to stop it and acquire the land, delaying the trail's development until 1990. The Forest Service also proved unsupportive. When Edwards asked the agency to take control and make trail improvements, the Black Hills Forest supervisor refused, stating that he wished to avoid financial obligations and liability issues. This decision frustrated Edwards, and he later reported that the supervisor was uncooperative, even refusing to attend public meetings.

These obstacles could have killed the trail, but Edwards found supporters who kept it alive. While South Dakota Game, Fish, and Parks had already expressed an interest in creating a trail, George S. Mickelson proved invaluable. During his campaign for the South Dakota governorship in 1986, Mickelson pledged to support the trail and have the state take control of the right-of-way. Once elected, he was true to his word. The state became the lead agency, working with the Burlington to transfer the right-of-way, defending the trail in court, and finding money to improve the route. Most importantly, Governors Mickelson and William Janklow directed hundreds of thousands of federal dollars to its construction under the 1991 Intermodal Surface Transportation Efficiency Act.

Once the South Dakota Supreme Court upheld a decision that allowed the state to take control of the right-of-way in 1990, actual construction began. Still, Edwards and others had to work diligently to find the money and manpower to improve the route. They sought private donations, which helped immensely, but several agencies were also crucial. Troops from the South Dakota National Guard rebuilt bridges, inmates from the Department of Corrections put up fences, and members of the South Dakota Mining Association volunteered their time. Also, a new Black Hills Forest supervisor reversed his predecessor's earlier stand and made the Forest Service a full-fledged partner, providing millions of dollars to build sections of the trail and rehabilitate four tunnels. Initial trail plans focused on the section from Hill City to Deadwood, but as the idea of establishing a trail developed, the state gained control of the entire branch line. The Burlington donated the section from Custer to Hill City to the state in 1988 and sold the Edgemont-to-Custer portion for $25,000 in 1990.

As work progressed throughout the 1990s, which included replacing nearly fifty trestles between Mystic and Deadwood, trail sections gradually opened. Governor Mickelson dedicated the first six miles in 1991, with more sections added in the years that followed. The 109-mile trail was completed in 1998 at an estimated cost of $5 million. It was initially called the Black Hills Burlington Northern Heritage Trail, but when Governor Mickelson and seven others were tragically killed in a plane crash in April 1993, it was renamed in his honor. For the trail to become a reality, key people, including Guy Edwards, Governor Mickelson, and Dave Snyder, worked long hours over many years. According to state park official Doug Hofer, Snyder's financial support and leadership in attracting other donations was critical to the trail's completion.

8.9 mi **Oreville Campground:** The Oreville name comes from an 1890 station on the Burlington Railroad. The railroad saw this location as a potential shipping point for tin and other pegmatite ores. Despite a number of mines opening and the construction of a small beryllium refining mill, Oreville never grew beyond a few residents. Today, Oreville is remembered with a campground and a Mickelson Trail rest shelter.

9.7 mi **Black Elk Peak View:** The trip north on US 385 offers a good view of Black Elk Peak, the Black Hills' highest mountain at 7,242 feet. While leading a topographical survey in 1857, Lieutenant Gouverneur K. Warren named the peak after General William S. Harney, a well-known military man and Warren's commander. Warren and his small contingent of men mostly stayed on the plains as they circled the Black Hills, and only saw the peak at a distance. The U.S. Board on Geographic Names voted to change the name in 2016. Harney had a reputation for savagery, coming in part from his attack on a Sicangu

Lakota camp on Blue Water Creek in Nebraska in 1855, for which the Lakotas named him "Woman Killer." The board renamed the peak to honor Lakota medicine man Nicholas Black Elk, the subject of John G. Neihardt's 1932 book about Lakota traditions, *Black Elk Speaks*.

13.3 mi **Take the Hill City US 16 Bypass/Truck route.**

13.5 mi **Turn right onto Poplar Street to reach the Mickelson Trailhead.**

13.6 mi **Charlotte Tracy Park, Mickelson Trailhead, Recommended Stop.**

Charlotte Tracy Park Cabin: Bill Tracy built this cabin in Allen Gulch about half a mile west of Hill City around 1890. It was later moved to this location and is called the oldest remaining building in Hill City, which may or may not be true. The park is named after Tracy's daughter.

Hill City History: Hill City, also known as Hillyo and Hilltown, is the second oldest community in the Black Hills. Gold was discovered along Spring Creek in late December 1875, quickly attracting 500 people, 250 houses, two stores, and a hotel. Like Custer, it boomed for a few months and then most of the residents rushed north to Deadwood Gulch. According to legend, only an old man and a dog remained. A small resurgence occurred in 1877 as miners returned to look for hardrock claims. They produced enough gold to keep Hill City alive. The discovery of tin in the 1880s brought more activity, but a real boom came in 1890 when the Burlington Railroad built to the town and the Harney Peak Tin Company placed its headquarters there. One observer counted fifteen saloons on Main Street, with another describing it as "a town with a church on each end and a mile of hell in between." The census reflects Hill City's booms and busts: the 1880 census showed no population, then in 1890 the census taker counted 479 people. A Black Hills newspaper from that time, however, estimated 1,200 residents, which may have been closer to the truth. But as the tin boom collapsed in the 1890s, the town had to rely

Hill City, viewed from the north, ca. fall 1891. In the foreground, on the right, is the Harney Peak Hotel, which was completed the following spring. *South Dakota State Historical Society*

on a few small hardrock gold mines, such as the J.R., the Golden Slipper, and the Sunbeam, and the intermittent output of a few pegmatite mines. The town's population dwindled from 602 people in 1900 to 213 in 1910 and neared zero in 1920. When a fire hit in 1902, newspapers reported that several of the destroyed buildings were empty.

1880 Train: Hill City saw a small recovery when Mount Rushmore and Custer State Park began attracting visitors in the 1930s. It got a bigger boost when Bill Heckman started the Black Hills Central Railroad (BHCRR), calling it the 1880 Train, in 1957. In an effort to emulate historic mountain railroading, Heckman laid a third rail between the existing standard gauge tracks to create a narrow gauge line for five miles from Hill City to Oblivion, a small stopover he built. Heckman used narrow gauge equipment until 1965, when he converted his operation to standard gauge and extended the tourist train to Keystone to attract more riders. While this brought extra business, Heckman seemed more interested in buying and selling equipment than in running a tourist attraction. The rail yard was littered with junk, and the tourist operation appeared shabby. At one time Heckman dreamed of creating an Old West town. After he acquired some western-looking structures, little happened. In 1990, Bob and Jo Anna Warder bought the property and turned it into a well-kept, well-run operation. They fixed up the equipment, cleaned the yards, and bought new motive power, including two large mallet steam locomotives. These engines attract rail fans from across the country. Today, the Warders' daughter, Meg, runs the tourist line.

South Dakota State Railroad Museum: The Warders are also responsible for the railroad museum. Not long after buying the 1880 Train, they officially organized a museum, but it was slow to develop. In 2004 they put artifacts in a Pullman rail car and in 2010 they built the current museum structure. Since the 1880 Train is the most viable tourist rail line in the state, Hill City seemed to be a natural location for a railroad museum, and the Warders convinced the legislature to recognize it as the "state" railroad museum. Still, people in such places as Aberdeen, which has a significant rail history, wondered why they should not have the state railroad museum. Although the museum is financially independent of the railroad, it uses railroad property, and the operating agreement limits what it can display outside as well as what its gift shop can sell. Some of the nation's more successful railroad museums have rail yards filled with equipment and depend on large gift shop sales. These limitations have hurt the museum's flexibility. Nevertheless, rail expert Rick Mills is the director and curator, and he has worked diligently to create a first-rate museum.

Hill City transformation: Much as the 1880 Train has changed over the years, Hill City has also been transformed. In the 1960s, the town was a mixture of rundown buildings, dirty streets, and garish novelty shops. One attraction was the Hill City "artist," who painted in an open-air stand on Main Street, using four-inch paint brushes and black felt canvas. In the 1990s, more established or sophisticated artists opened studios, turning the town into an art center. Because he primarily paints Black Hills scenes, Jon Crane is probably the most famous. He opened a gallery in 1995 and moved to his current location in 1998. Besides becoming a vibrant art community, Hill

The Central Black Hills Railroad's 1880 train, during a special excursion with two mallet steam engines, 20 August 2022. *Author photo*

City has attracted other upscale shops that have added to the town's transformation.

Historic Hill City Main Street locations: The four locations discussed below are on the left, or west, side of Main Street.

***Harney Peak Mining News* Building (1885), 301 Main Street:** Using long hand-hewn logs, German immigrant Camillo Von Woehrmann constructed the building at the corner of Main and McGregor Streets for a saloon and sleeping quarters in about 1885. He converted it into a newspaper office in 1890 and published the *Harney Peak Mining News* until he returned to Germany in 1922. After his departure, the structure housed a variety of businesses, including a night club, a car garage, and a fly-fishing shop. During these years, it was expanded and remodeled, including the application of stucco to

The D.B. Ingram & C. McEachron general store in Hill City, ca. 1885.
Watson Parker Ghost Town Notebooks, Leland D. Case Library for Western Historical Studies, Black Hills State University

the walls. It survived Hill City fires in 1891 and 1902 and a building fire in 1975. The last blaze, however, revealed the log structure hidden underneath the stucco. The owners decided to restore the logs, and after some investigation determined that it is the oldest commercial hand-hewn log building in South Dakota. The building has recently housed a restaurant.

C. E. McEachron General Merchandise Building (1902), 261 Main Street: Charles E. McEachron came to the Black Hills from New York around 1879. He worked on the Rockerville Flume for a time, then opened a general merchandise store at this location as Hill City experienced a small boom in 1890. After a 1902 fire destroyed his wood building, he built this large, two-story brick structure. For years it stood out as Hill City's biggest commercial front. McEachron stayed in business until the late 1920s. The building has since housed a variety of businesses, including a music venue known as Lit'l Nashville and an art gallery. It is currently home to a Harley-Davidson store.

The Alpine Inn, 133 Main Street: The Alpine Inn is a Hill City landmark. The restaurant has become famous for its cuisine. The building is a tangible reminder of the Harney Peak Tin Company, which built it in the late 1880s and early 1890s. Harney Peak Tin is more thoroughly discussed at the Keystone stop.

The Black Hills Institute of Geological Research, 117 Main Street: In a remodeled gymnasium on the same block as the Alpine Inn is the Black Hills Institute. Two paleontologists, brothers Neal and Peter Larson, opened the institute in 1974. While they hired out for paleontological digs, they also explored on their own, hoping to make a big find. Most famously, while excavating near Faith, South Dakota, on the Cheyenne River Indian Reservation, in 1990, they uncovered Sue, the most complete Tyrannosaurus Rex fossil ever found, and named it after the person who made the find, Sue Hendrickson. Peter Larson paid the property owner the $5,000 he requested and brought the fossil to Hill City. Many entities soon laid claim to the T. Rex, however, including the property owner, the BIA, and the FBI. During the fight, the U.S. attorney for South Dakota had the National Guard haul Sue away in 1992. After a ten-year court battle, the property owner won claim to Sue and put it up for auction. Chicago's Field Museum bought the fossil for $8.4 million. In the process, Peter Larson was sent to jail for eighteen months on unrelated charges. CNN distributed a documentary called *Dinosaur 13* about Sue and the surrounding events.

Stan: The Larson brothers discovered another T. Rex, Stan, just outside of Buffalo, South Dakota, in 1987 and unearthed it in 1992. Though not as complete as Sue, Stan is the second-most complete T. Rex and has the most perfectly preserved skull ever found. That made the discovery valuable, and Stan became the centerpiece of the Black Hills Institute's collection. A number of museums and collectors wanted to view Stan's skull, so the institute started selling castings for $100,000 each. It also rented castings for $20,000 a month. Stan has become the most duplicated dinosaur fossil in existence. The Institute used the revenue to fund more fossil hunts and for other expenses. Sadly, a dispute between the brothers resulted in lawsuits. In the end, a judge ordered the institute's assets divided equally. Peter got the institute and the rights to Stan's castings, while Neal got Stan. The judge estimated the institute's worth at $5 million; Stan was estimated to be worth $6–8 million. Neal sold Stan to an anonymous bidder at an October 2020 auction for $31.8 million, the highest price ever paid for a fossil. As Peter said, "That's more than we've grossed in the entire history of our business." Peter has since restructured the institute.

Part Four Keystone Mining Country

This portion of the Gold Rush Tour takes a side trip to Keystone. While prospectors explored the creeks in the Keystone area early in the gold rush, the town developed well after the gold rush ended. In fact, the excitement of the Harney Peak Tin boom had already come and gone by the time Keystone was founded. Nevertheless, it was a mining town, ultimately producing a significant amount of gold and other minerals.

Route Overview: From Tracy Park turn onto Poplar Street, then right onto Railroad Avenue. Follow Railroad Avenue until it merges with US 16/385. Immediately after the roads merge, turn right onto Old Hill City Road, County Road 323, and follow it into Historic Keystone for a Recommended Stop.

Mileage starts at Tracy Park.

0.0 mi **Tracy Park: Turn onto Poplar Street.**

0.1 mi **Turn right onto Railroad Avenue, the Hill City bypass.**

0.4 mi **Merge with US 16/385.**

0.5 mi **Turn toward Keystone onto Old Hill City Road, County Road 323.**

0.5 mi **Keystone Railroad Spur:** The railroad branch line that ran between Hill City and Keystone got its start when the Burlington Railroad built a four-mile spur from Hill City to the Harney Peak Tin Company's Addie Mine and Camp in 1892. The rail line's primary purpose was to haul tin ore from the mine to the company's mill in Hill City, but there was very little ore. The Burlington then extended its track to Keystone to serve the Holy Terror, Keystone, and Bullion gold mines in February 1900. Once these mines shut down, the rail

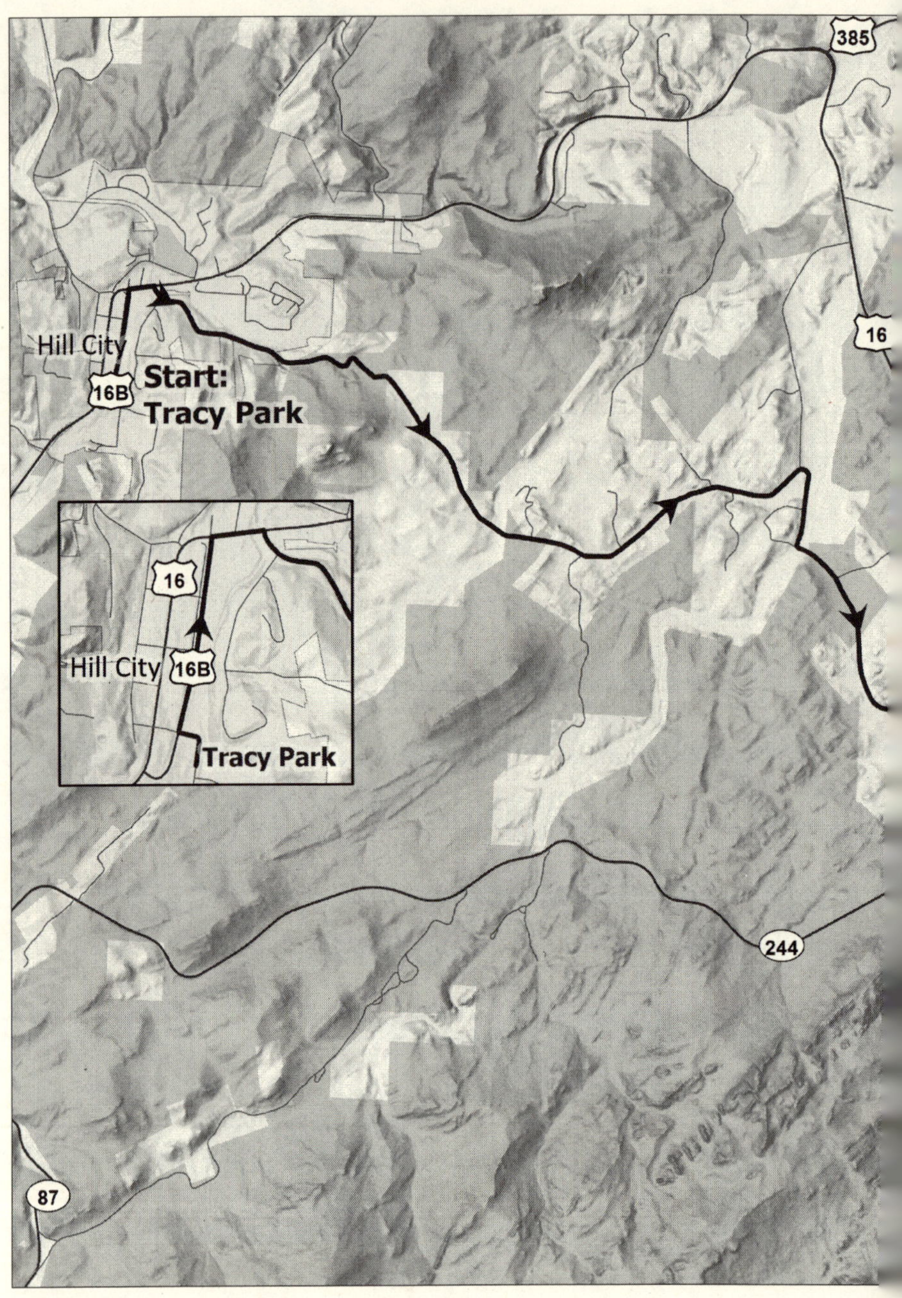
385
16
Hill City
16B
Start:
Tracy Park
16
Hill City
16B
Tracy Park
244
87

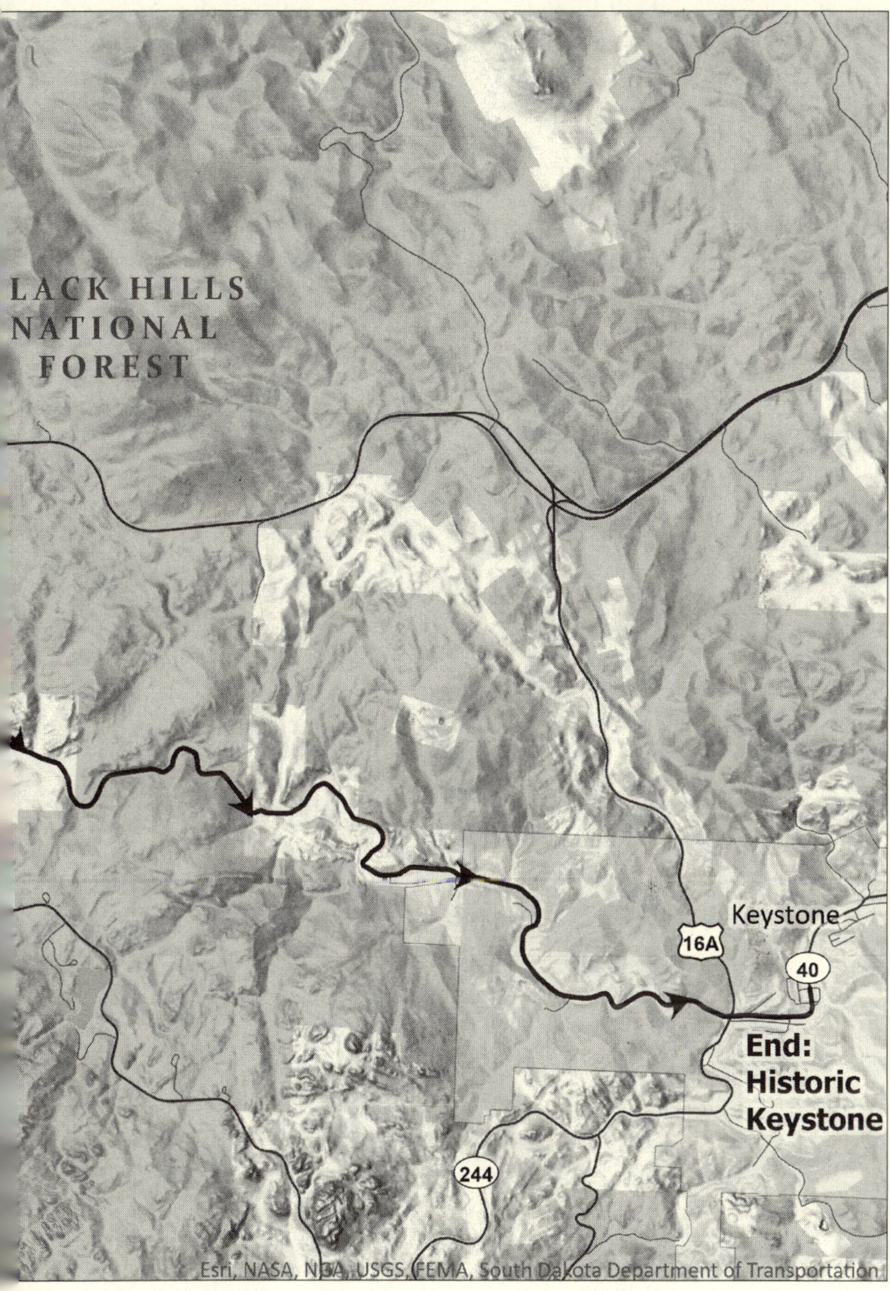
LACK HILLS
NATIONAL
FOREST
Keystone
16A
40
End:
Historic
Keystone
244
Esri, NASA, NGA, USGS, FEMA, South Dakota Department of Transportation

company's main products became feldspar, beryllium, spodumene, and arsenic. Despite limited traffic, the Burlington operated the Keystone branch until a flood on Battle Creek took out part of the track in 1972. The 1880 Train, however, has kept the branch line alive, including repairing the flood damage.

1.4 mi **Tin Mill Hill:** The road out of Hill City goes up Tin Mill Hill. A railroad spur at the top of the hill served the Harney Peak Tin Company's processing plant.

2.9 mi **Palmer Gulch Road:** Prospectors George Palmer, John Brennan, and others found small amounts of gold in Palmer Gulch in late 1875. They soon became disenchanted and set out for the plains, where they founded Rapid City in February 1876, envisioning a mining service center there, a "Denver of the Black Hills."

3.1 mi **Tin Lode Court:** Some roads still honor the area's mining past with such names as Tin Lode Court and Wolframite Road. Wolframite is a pegmatite mineral valued for its tungsten content.

3.3 mi **Addie Camp:** A neglected two-story house on the left (north) of the road is known as the Kennedy or Canaday House. It once housed a bar and grocery store for the mining camp of Kennedyville or Addie Camp. Harney Peak Tin dug an 800-foot shaft at Addie. The mine, however, produced little of value. Besides the Kennedy House, the small town also had a boarding house and a few scattered residences. Once the mine closed, it became a farming community.

3.6 mi **Iron Horse Court:** The Burlington's 1892 spur to the Addie Tin Mine sat very close to Iron Horse Court. The tracks were taken up in 1917.

4.0 mi **American Tungsten Mining Co.:** On the right-hand side, on the hill within the road's sharp curve, are the remains of a processing plant built by the American Tungsten Mining Company in 1907. The company owned the Success and Good Luck claims, which had a variety of pegmatite minerals, but it mined tungsten because of its importance in making steel. After producing a small amount of tungsten, the operation closed. Tungsten demand increased as World War II approached, causing General Electric to recondition the mill. It was abandoned again after the war.

4.3 mi **Watson Parker Road and Kennedyville Loop:** The Kennedyville Loop was named after the town that once sat across the road. Watson Parker Road was named after a noted Black Hills historian. The Parker family owned a large amount of land along Palmer Creek and a summer retreat known as Palmer Gulch Lodge just below Mount Rushmore. A KOA campground occupies the resort's location today. Parker family members still have summer homes and a private cemetery along Watson Parker Road.

7.7 mi **Pine Camp/Camp Judson:** The Harney Peak Tin Co. established an office at Pine Camp near this location in 1885. The company and the camp, however, did not last long. Pine Camp came back to life when the Burlington extended its line from Addie Camp to Keystone in 1900. It first served as a railroad construction camp and then as a lumber camp. Chris Overgaard opened a sawmill there in 1916 and ran it until the Great Depression forced him to close. The Baptist Church eventually obtained the site and opened a summer retreat known as Camp Judson in 1955. It replaced a Camp Judson that the church had established near the town of Pactola on Rapid Creek in the 1920s. The Bureau of Reclamation purchased the camp when it constructed Pactola Dam.

8.8 mi **The Ingersoll Mine:** High on the hill to the east, out of sight from the road, is the Ingersoll pegmatite mine. The mine was named for Bob Ingersoll, a famous lawyer, politician, and orator who died in 1899. He was known as a free thinker and called "the Great Agnostic." The Harney Peak Tin Co. owned the mine in the 1880s but did little mining. Other owners followed, operating the mine intermittently from 1922 to 1956. The mine produced mica, spodumene, feldspar, and beryl. Sometimes valued as a gemstone, beryl was used as an alloy with other metals to add strength. A large mill building dating from 1942 once stood here, and despite the owners discouraging visi-

The Ingersoll Mine in 2008. It was destroyed by a fire in 2022. *Author photo*

tors, it became a popular hiking destination. Sadly, it was destroyed by a fire in February 2022.

9.8 mi **Lafferty Gulch:** The Dan Patch pegmatite mine sat near Lafferty Gulch. It produced feldspar and mica from 1939 to 1942. A large open pit remains, but access is blocked.

10.5 mi **Junction of Old Hill City Road and US 16A: Cross US 16A and continue into old Keystone.**

11.2 mi **Recommended Stop in old Keystone:**
Pull into the small dirt lot next to the "Rock Shed," in front of the ruins of the Keystone and Holy Terror Mines.
Keystone: The town has two parts: historic "old Keystone" and the more recent tourist section. This part of the tour focuses on old Keystone.

When compared to other Black Hills gold towns, Keystone was a latecomer. It was founded in 1892, after prospectors discovered the Keystone Mine. Still, much happened in the area before it was founded, especially along Battle Creek, which flows through the old part of town, and Grizzly or Grizzly Bear Creek, which flows through new Keystone.

Early Prospectors: Prospectors searched for gold along Battle, Grizzly Bear, and Iron Creeks as early as 1875, and discovered small amounts in Battle Creek. In fact, Walter P. Jenney, of the 1875 Newton–Jenney Expedition, claimed to have pulled up a rose bush near Battle Creek and shook fifty cents of gold from its roots. Some of these discoveries were made close to the plains, which meant Lakotas were close by. One story even tells of warriors firing on a group of miners as they gathered around a campfire. None were hurt, but a bullet passed through their frying pan, persuading them to leave.

Hayward: One group of miners established a camp on Battle Creek about five and a half miles below Keystone in November 1876, naming it after Charles Hayward, one of its members. The gold they found was deeply buried, and the shafts they dug to reach it occasionally flooded. At other times Battle Creek had too little water to run placer equipment. To solve these problems, the prospectors dammed the creek and ran the stored water through hydraulic mining equipment to wash away overburden and expose the gold. In 1878, two hydraulic companies formed, the Iron Creek Flume and Mining Company and the Battle Creek Flume and Mining Company. Reports of rich finds were just wishful thinking. Still, other companies followed. The Battle Creek Gravel Mining Company built dams and flumes in 1880, but it also failed to produce gold.

Custer County Seat: When the territorial legislature created Custer County, the newly appointed county commissioners selected Hayward as the county seat in April 1877. But as mining stalled and people left in 1878 and 1879, residents of Custer City wanted the county seat moved. The issue was placed on the 4 November 1879 ballot and Custer won. To ensure the county seat's permanence, Custer residents built a courthouse in 1881. A survey that same year showed that Hayward was actually in Pennington County, ending any chance of it reclaiming the county seat.

One story claims that Custer residents, anxious for the county seat, stole the records soon after the election. The thieves were quickly caught and forced to return the documents. Custer had to wait until the official transfer date. Tales such as this one are commonly told about county seat fights, which brings the veracity of this account into question.

Hayward Today: Hayward hung on for a few years after 1880. While the town no longer exists, it is home to Rushmore Cave. Miners reportedly discovered the cave while searching for a leak in one of their flumes in 1880, but they paid little attention to it. Local residents also showed little interest until some young people discovered previously unknown chambers in the 1920s. The owners then decided to open the cave for tours in 1927 and changed its name from Hayward Cave to Rushmore Cave to capitalize on the publicity surrounding the dedication and early work on Mount Rushmore. The current proprietors not only offer tours but have also added a zip line and a rollercoaster. These amusements seem to appeal to a new generation of tourists who want more excitement than can be found in the natural wonder of a cave.

Harney: The camp of Harney sat two miles below Keystone on Battle Creek. It was laid out in 1876 but abandoned by 1878. Its story is similar to Hayward's: water problems seemingly prevented the recovery of gold, if any existed. Entrepreneurs occasionally tried to recover it, or at least convinced gullible investors to spend money on trying. In 1881, a company known as Harney (or Harney Peak) Hydraulic began building a long flume. It was supposed to channel water from both Grizzly Bear and Battle Creeks in a trestle 700 feet long and 200 feet high, to be built toward Harney through where Keystone is today. The promoters' goal was to create enough water pressure to uncover gold for about six miles along Battle Creek. After a year and a half, the operators had little to show for their efforts, and the investors finally saw it as a fraud. Harney was again deserted. Today there are only a few homes in the area.

Harney Peak Tin: Tin mining brought significant activity to the Keystone area, primarily along Grizzly Bear or Grizzly Gulch, closer to new Keystone. It began in 1883 when A. J. Simmons sent a sample of ore from the Etta Mine to an expert, asking for a "determination." William Blake, a respected mining man, did the analysis in California, reporting over 75 percent metallic tin. He soon labeled the hill "Tin Mountain." This was a big deal as the United States had no paying quantities of tin and imported up to $24 million of the metal from Great Britain each year. Reports circulated that "these mines will certainly rule the tin market of the world." Simmons sold his interest to businesspeople in New York for what one paper called a "handsome consideration" in June 1884. The New York investors then organized the Harney Peak Tin Mining, Milling and Manufacturing Company.

The company began developing the mine and expanding its holdings. It bought claims throughout the area and built a mill near the Etta Mine in 1886. A small town known as Stanum sprang up. But as it transpired, Simmons had sold investors a tin mine with little tin. Whether he knew that is unclear. He had a good reputation and would later serve as mayor of Rapid City, but he was "always an optimist" and was involved in several mining enterprises, some of which turned out to be failures and possibly frauds.

After the initial failure, the owners proclaimed that the first results were not indicative of what existed. Other samples showed "admirable" returns and an important source of tin. The directors also began selling stock in London, with influential British investors joining the board of a reorganized company beginning in 1887. There were many critics of the company. The *Engineering and Mining Journal* speculated that it was reorganized so the New York shareholders could unload worthless stock. In any case, the new Harney Peak Tin Company bought more property. By 1892, it had 1,100 mining claims. With each claim representing a little over ten acres, it controlled about 11,000 acres of land, and the company went on a building spree. It refitted the Etta mill, constructed hoisting plants at its five principal mines, and built several new structures around Hill City, including a 250-ton mill, boardinghouses, blacksmith shops, carpenter shops, machine shops, an office, the Alpine Inn, a foundry, and storehouses. The monthly payroll reportedly totaled $30,000.

After operating for about two months, in February 1893 the Hill City mill shut down, with little tin recovered, putting 400 men out of work. The New York interests had indeed perpetrated a fraud. They had duped the London shareholders into investing an estimated $3 million in a company that produced only $1,545 worth of tin. The fiasco became internationally infamous.

The only positive outcome was the Alpine Inn. As the inn's website states, the company "spent millions of unseen investor's dollars boosting the town's economy," while encouraging the Burlington Railroad to build through Hill City in 1890.

The founding of Keystone: Although placer mining, flume building, and tin speculation occurred in the area, little development occurred along this section of Battle Creek, except for the construction of a few stores and cabins, until three prospectors staked the Keystone claim in 1891. One of them, Jacob Reed, also located the Reed Placer Claim along Battle Creek and platted the town of Keystone on his claim in 1892.

Holy Terror: Keystone began to prosper when William Franklin, known as Rocky Mountain Frank, accidentally discovered the Holy Terror Mine in 1894. Many stories exist about the mine's discovery, but one version has Franklin and his daughter picking strawberries on the side of Mount Aetna, on Keystone's west side. While resting, something bright caught the young lady's eye. She called her father over, and he recognized gold. Franklin promptly staked a claim, naming it the Holy Terror, reportedly "honoring" his wife. It soon became, as a Department of the Interior publication states, "one of the most famous mines in the Black Hills." Franklin and a partner dug a shaft and soon hit abundant high-grade, free-milling gold ore, which could be readily treated by available processes. In fact, gold could be seen protruding from the native quartz. The Holy Terror and the Homestake were about the only two mines in the Black Hills that had abundant free-milling ore; the Holy Terror ore was valued at $500 per ton. As Franklin and his partner brought in other investors, they built a small stamp mill and began producing $10,000 per week, which attracted national attention. After a year, they sold out. The new owners deepened the shaft and erected a larger mill. One author states that as gold production increased, the Holy Terror became the anchor of the southern Black Hills' economy and "brought dignity" to a

William Franklin, also known as "Rocky Mountain Frank," discoverer of the Holy Terror Mine. *South Dakota State Historical Society*

Workers in the Holy Terror Mine, undated. *Black Hills Historical Society*

region whose reputation had been damaged by the Harney Peak Tin scandal.

In 1898 the owners of the Holy Terror and the Keystone Mines consolidated operations, driving tunnels between the two properties. Reports claim that $570,000 in gold was produced in 1898–1899. The mines were forced to close in 1903. The troubles began when the shaft flooded and the company struggled to dewater it. Then an explosion and fire killed three miners and injured seventeen others. Litigation followed, with the company losing several expensive lawsuits. In the years after, the mine operated intermittently. A new mill went up in 1929, but it burned. Another was built in 1939, but the government ordered gold mines closed during World War II and it never reopened. The Holy Terror and Keystone Mines produced an estimated $1.3 million in gold.

Bullion Mine: The Bullion Mine sat just east of the Keystone–Holy Terror complex. It carried gold and silver, but it also contained sulfides and arsenides, making the ore difficult to treat and profits elusive. A boll weevil infestation in southern cotton fields reversed the Bullion's fortunes in 1924. With arsenic in demand, the mine owners sent ore to the Globe smelter in Denver for treatment. When the smelter successfully recovered nearly 50 tons of arsenic, the Bullion built a processing plant at the mine site. Just as the price of arsenic had gone up quickly, it went down quickly, and the plant soon closed. Efforts to recover gold also failed, and the mine was done by 1930.

Other prospects: Several claims were staked across the valley from the Holy Terror, but few prospered. The Columbia dug a 300-foot shaft and produced some gold from a small but seemingly rich vein. The Lucky Boy also had a 300-foot shaft but showed no results. Keystone's most famous mine may be the Big Thunder, which has been a heavily promoted tourist attraction since the 1960s. It is located on the Reed Placer claim, the same claim as the town. Two German immigrants dug what was called the Krupp Tunnel at that location in 1892 or 1893, but there is no record of production.

Pegmatite Mining: The 1920s brought new mining activity to the area when prices for the minerals found in pegmatite ores went up. Mines such as the Peerless, the Hugo, and the Etta opened. Most of these were located closer to Grizzly Bear Creek, near new Keystone, but a feldspar-grinding plant was built along the railroad in 1928, near the junction of Grizzly Bear and Battle Creeks, just above old Keystone. It burned in 1957.

Recent gold activity: An advance in gold prices brought renewed attention to the Keystone area. In the 1990s, a company drilled sixty test holes, without going into production, and from 2012 to 2015, Mineral Mountain Mining signed an exploration agreement with the owners of the Holy Terror. This Toronto-based company bought several other claims. It drilled forty test holes but went no further. While the operators apparently found gold, they felt it was not practical to mine at the time. They could return if conditions become more favorable. After leaving Keystone, Mineral Mountain began exploring around Rochford in 2018.

The Burlington Railroad: The Burlington built into Keystone from Hill City to serve the Holy Terror, Keystone, and Bullion Mines in 1900. With the Holy Terror–Keystone closing in 1903, the spur had little traffic. Its main products became feldspar, beryllium, spodumene, and arsenic. The railroad continued operations on the branch until the 1972 Black Hills flood severely damaged the track.

1880 Train: The Black Hills Central Railroad (BHCRR) began running excursions into Keystone when it changed from narrow gauge to standard gauge operations in 1965. After the 1972 flood destroyed the track, trains stopped at what was called Keystone Junction, a little distance from town on the Old Hill City Road. The BHCRR owners eventually reconstructed the line to Keystone to better capitalize on tourist traffic.

Mount Rushmore: When Gutzon Borglum selected nearby Mount Rushmore to carve his monument, Keystone residents recognized the potential benefits. To make sure their town sat on the path to the mountain, they used axes, shovels, and horse-drawn scrapers to open a "passable" road in time for Borglum's 1925 dedication. They also arranged to have horses and teamsters stationed along the route to help faltering automobiles. Locals may have also opened the first Rushmore-related concession when they sold barbecue elk sandwiches at the Congregational church. For lack of funding, little happened at the mountain until President Coolidge came to town for a 1927 dedication. The president's limousine stopped at a pool hall where he drank a bottle of soda. With western imagery in mind, he mounted a horse and led his entourage to Mount Rushmore. After Coolidge's visit, work on the monument began in earnest. Despite occasional shutdowns when funds ran out, between twenty-five and thirty former Keystone miners found work at the monument, and other Rushmore employees moved to town, finding plenty of empty houses to choose from. The old mining camp also served as the project's supply center. The railroad delivered supplies, and the Keystone Consolidated Mines, which controlled the Holy Terror, provided power.

Keystone in Good Times and Bad: During mining's heyday, the town was a vibrant community, with a population of around 2,000 in the 1890s. It had a variety of businesses, including a reported sixteen saloons. But as the mines closed and people left, only about 300 residents remained. The business district similarly disappeared, mainly from fires—four hit town between 1908 and 1937. Because of the losses, few historic structures remain. One exception is the old Keystone School on the slope of Mount Aetna. Built in 1899, it served as a school until 1988, with its athletic teams known as the "Dynamiters." It is now a museum. Another historic property is Halley's General Store. Dating from 1896, it is Keystone's oldest continuously operated business. The store's name comes from James Halley III, who purchased it in 1917. His grandfather, James Halley I, was a prominent Rapid City citizen, serving as mayor and bank president.

Famous Resident, Caroline Ingalls Swanzey: A younger sister of author Laura Ingalls Wilder, Caroline Ingalls Swanzey lived in Keystone for over three decades. In addition to proving up on a

The Halley General Store in Keystone, 2022. *Author photo*

homesteading claim outside Topbar, South Dakota, she had mastered the newspaper trade. She arrived in Keystone in 1911 to manage the *Keystone Recorder*, owned by the news magnate E. L. Senn. She also worked for the *Hill City Star*. The following year she married David Swanzey and quit her job to care for his children and her blind sister, Mary. Swanzey had come to the area before Keystone existed and staked a placer claim on Grizzly Bear Creek, where the Roosevelt Inn is today located in new Keystone. Besides prospecting, he worked odd jobs. In 1885, he and another man guided New York attorney Charles Rushmore on his inspection of Harney Peak Tin Company properties. It was during this trip that Swanzey reportedly named Mount Rushmore after his client. When the Burlington built to town, Swanzey became a station agent. He died in 1938 at the age of eighty-three. Swanzey Street is named after him. After his death, Caroline remained in Keystone until she passed away in 1946.

Famous Residents, The Bower Family Band: The Bower Family Band was composed of John ("Cal") and Keziah ("Kizzie") Bower and their seven children (five girls and two boys). They had formed the brass band in 1884 while living in Vermillion, but moved to the

Black Hills soon after, perhaps to be closer to their daughter Alice, who had married Joseph Gossage, the owner of the *Rapid City Journal,* in 1882. Family members established homesteads on Battle and French Creeks and started giving concerts around the Black Hills. In the years that followed, the children took jobs throughout the Black Hills, and some got married. Even so, the band still gathered to perform. When Cal moved to Keystone in 1895, during the Holy Terror boom, several children followed. This allowed them to perform until the mine closed and the family moved away. In 1961, the youngest daughter, Laura Bower Van Nuys, now married to a professor at the South Dakota School of Mines, wrote *The Family Band: From the Missouri to the Black Hills, 1881–1900,* which was later adapted into a 1968 Disney movie, *The One and Only, Genuine, Original Family Band.*

Glendale: The gold, tin, and pegmatite mining that took place in Keystone also occurred in Glendale, a mile south of the former gold camp of Harney on Iron Creek. Prospectors reportedly found gold in Iron Creek, but little came of it. Promoters talked of building a flume through the area, primarily to carry water to mining operations on Battle Creek. In the early 1880s a prospector found tin in what was called the Otho Mine. The Glendale Mining Company of Chicago bought the claims in 1889 and built a 150-ton mill. Like other mines in the area, it failed to produce tin, and closed by 1891. Another company took over in 1892 and unsuccessfully looked for gold. In 1913, the property was refurbished and a new mill was installed to process pegmatites such as beryl and feldspar. It ran intermittently over the years, lasting until 1939. Some of the buildings survived, and a couple of Keystone businesspeople eventually remodeled them for the Meeting the Need camp, which opened for people with disabilities in 2005.

Part Five Following the Gold Rush North

Route Overview: Drive through old Keystone toward US 16A. At the stoplight, turn right and travel north on US 16A. At the intersection with US 16, merge onto the westbound lane toward Hill City. At the junction of US 16 with US 385, turn right (north) onto US 385, and continue to Sheridan Lake for a Recommended Stop.

Mileage starts at Holy Terror Mine pull-off.

0.0 mi **Holy Terror Mine pullout: Return to US 16A.**

0.5 mi **Intersection with US 16A at stoplight. Turn right (north).**

1.5 mi **Bismarck Mine:** Prospectors discovered outcroppings of the Keystone gold belt on the mountain to the right (south), where the Bismarck and Ida Florence Mines opened in 1893. They were worked intermittently until 1936. Existing records indicate that the mines produced just over 1,000 ounces of gold. Mineral Mountain Mining of Canada explored the property from 2012 to 2015, but no further work has been done as of 2023.

1.7 mi **Powder House Lodge:** This tourist stop sits directly across the valley from the Bismarck and Ida Florence Mines. The lodge owners state that a small log building once stood there, used to store blasting powder, no doubt associated with the nearby mines.

2.8 mi **Junction of US 16A & US 16. Angle to the left and take US 16 to the left (west).** The highway crosses a highway interchange known as the Keystone WYE. The interchange features two bridges, with six arching beams made from glued, laminated lumber supporting the top bridge. The WYE was constructed in 1967–1968 when the Department of Transportation widened the road. The designers wanted to build a structure with a pleasing design that complemented the natural environment.

End:
Sheridan Lake
385
Three Forks
385
16
BLACK HILLS
NATIONAL
FOREST
16
16A
244
Keyston
40
Start: Historic Keysto

7.6 mi **Golden Slipper Road:** This road's name refers to a nearby mine. Prospectors explored the area early in the gold rush, but it was not until the 1890s that a small number of mines opened, including the J.R., the J.R. Extension, the Golden Summit, and the Golden Slipper. Of these, the Golden Slipper may have been the most successful, producing $46,000 in gold between 1893 and 1899. The mines were worked intermittently in the early twentieth century, especially during the Depression, but little has been done since.

8.3 mi **Junction of US 16 & US 385. Take US 385 to the right (north).** Once the tour turns onto US 385, it again meets Spring Creek. It was along this creek, near Hill City, that prospectors made the rush's second discovery. After that find, gold seekers followed Spring Creek northward, detecting gold as they went.

Known as Three Forks Junction, various businesses have served travelers at this location, such as the "3 Forks Inn, Motor Lodge" in the 1960s.

10.2 mi **Recommended Stop at the Sheridan Lake pull-off:** An interpretative sign at the pull-off helps explain the area's history. Sheridan Lake is fed by Spring Creek, one of the four creeks in the southern and central Black Hills that carried gold (the other three were French, Castle, and Rapid Creeks). This diminutive creek flows through Hill City, fills Mitchell and Sheridan Lakes, passes Reptile Gardens, and then exits the Black Hills running through Hart Ranch, eventually draining into the Cheyenne River.

Golden City: Prospectors discovered gold along Spring Creek in the summer of 1875, but General Crook quickly removed most of these trespassers. In early 1876, soon after the army quit guarding the Black Hills, the gold diggers returned and established Golden City. With the usual mix of saloons, gambling halls, and general stores, Golden City was the third camp founded in the Black Hills, following Hill City and Custer City. Despite the name, the gold proved spotty. Some claims yielded good amounts of gold, while others produced nothing. A group from Montana reportedly took out $1,600 in March 1876, and another claim owner found enough gold to attract claim jumpers. He had to hold them off with a shotgun, and his location became known as Stand-off Bar. As with Custer City and Hill City, before long most of the prospectors left for Deadwood Gulch, though some stayed behind.

Sheridan: As people trickled back hoping to find undiscovered wealth in 1877, Golden City gained new life and the residents changed its name to Sheridan, after Civil War hero General Philip H. Sheridan. Now in command of the Military Division of the Missouri, he had purview over the Black Hills. Naming the town after the general may have been a way to honor him, but it was more likely a ploy to win political support. A group of Dakota Territory politicians had acquired land around Sheridan and formed the Black Hills Town Company with the goal of selling it at a profit. Dakota Territory governor John L. Pennington and congressional delegate Jefferson Parish Kidder were apparently involved, and they persuaded President Rutherford B. Hayes to place the U.S. Land Office in the town in March 1877. In April, when the legislature created Pennington County, Sheridan became the county seat. The Yankton and Deadwood papers damned these actions as political tricks, with one article stating that the operatives were part of a political ring. The plan soon collapsed anyway. Complaints from Deadwood convinced the commissioner of the General Land Office to move the Black Hills office there in late 1877,

The Pennington County Courthouse, 1876. *Watson Parker Ghost Town Notebooks, Leland D. Case Library for Western Historical Studies, Black Hills State University*

and Pennington County voters chose Rapid City as the new county seat in November.

In October 1877, prior to losing its prominence, Sheridan had the honor of hosting the first term of the district court in the Black Hills, with federal judge Granville Bennett presiding. Because of the number of cases affecting Deadwood, many people made the trip, including those who just wanted "to see the fun." The visitors even imported an entire saloon. Sheridan was overwhelmed, forcing people to sleep wherever they could, including on the floor of the log cabin courthouse. Nevertheless, Bennett held court without a problem, and the log cabin became known as the Black Hills' "first courthouse." A crude sign stating that fact was later placed in front of the building. A fire destroyed the cabin in 1895.

A wagon road and a few nearby gold mines provided some business for the struggling camp. Local optimists also dreamed of developing area copper deposits. The 1875 Newton–Jenney Expedition had identified copper outcroppings in the mountain that sits just east of today's Sheridan Lake, earning it the name Blue Lead Mountain. Over the years, several people tried to recover the copper, which included building a small smelter. The most famous operation was the Dakota–Calumet. In the end, little copper was produced, but the miners left numerous small tunnels and a shaft. With copper mines in Michigan and Montana dominating the market, any copper operation would have struggled to compete.

Rockerville: This gold camp sat several miles east of Sheridan, but residents still watched its development with interest. Gold was discovered along a branch of Spring Creek in 1876, but a lack of water made it difficult to recover. The camp eventually became known as Rockerville, named after a piece of mining equipment that could recover gold with little water: the "rocker" or "rocker box." The claim owners, however, wanted better results and decided to build a flume to transport water from Spring Creek, near Sheridan, to Rockerville. It took from 1878 to 1880 to build the seventeen-mile flume, and although it leaked, it worked well enough to allow for hydraulic mining, in which water pressure is used to wash away overburden and expose

Hydraulic mining near Rockerville, ca. 1880s. *Library of Congress*

the gold. About $500,000 of gold was recovered before it closed. The flume's legacy lives on; its path has been turned into one of the Black Hills' most popular hiking trails. The trail may be accessed on the east side of Sheridan Lake.

Logging: Timber harvesting came to the Sheridan area in 1908 when the Lanphere-Hinrichs Lumber Company built a railroad into the Victoria Creek drainage, about five miles northeast of Sheridan, and began harvesting trees for its Rapid City sawmill. The Warren-Lamb Company bought Lanphere-Hinrichs in 1914 and moved the timber operations to Custer State Park. They returned to the Sheridan area in 1926 and built a railroad spur into the Spring Creek drainage and eventually through where Sheridan Lake is today. Warren-Lamb abandoned rail operations and turned to trucks when the CCC began constructing the dam in 1938. The company continued logging until its sawmill burned in 1954. Evidence of the railroad's bed remains along Spring Creek.

Sheridan Lake: Sheridan Lake, like most Black Hills lakes, was a New Deal project. In 1937, a variety of agencies, including the Forest Service, the South Dakota Game Commission, the Izaak Walton League (an environmental organization founded in 1922 to promote natural resource protection and outdoor recreation), and federal relief programs, developed a plan to dam Spring Creek and create a 400-acre lake. To generate interest in the project, officials held a naming contest. The winner was "Lake o' the Pines," but most people continued calling it Sheridan Lake, and the new name was soon dropped. CCC workers, under Forest Service supervision, finished the dam in 1941, creating the largest CCC-built lake in the Black Hills. Sadly, twenty feet of water covered the former gold camp. The U.S. Forest Service still owns the lake, and unlike dams controlled by the U.S. Army Corps of Engineers and the Bureau of Reclamation, there is no domestic or industrial call on the water. Instead, it is dedicated to recreation and to maintaining Spring Creek's fishery. Hence, the water level is fairly stable throughout the year.

Part Six The Gold Rush on Rapid Creek

Route Overview: From Sheridan Lake, travel north on US 385 to Pactola Lake for a Recommended Stop.

Mileage starts at Sheridan Lake.

0.0 mi **Sheridan Lake: Return to US 385 and travel north.**

2.3 mi **Camp 15:** This road's name is a reminder of the area's logging past. The Warren-Lamb Lumber Company established many remote logging camps to supply its Rapid City sawmill in the early twentieth century. Like most logging companies, instead of applying names to these temporary locations, Warren-Lamb just numbered them sequentially. "Camp 15" was up this road. A few other Black Hills roads carry similar names and often refer to former logging sites.

5.5 mi **Black Forest Inn:** The road to the west, Forest Service Road 258, goes to a bed & breakfast known as the Black Forest Inn. Bernice Musekamp built the large log structure in 1953–1954 to replace a lodge and restaurant that she had operated at the townsite of Pactola since 1937. The construction of Pactola Dam forced her to relocate. She used the same name at both locations: Moosecamp Lodge. Carl and Kay Burgess renamed it the Black Forest Inn after purchasing the lodge from Musekamp in 1962. The building has since been sold and remodeled.

7.7 mi **Bullock Lookout:** In the far distance to the west is a fire tower named after Seth Bullock, a pioneer sheriff and early Black Hills Forest supervisor. The lookout sits on 5,922-foot Scruton Mountain, named for two brothers who owned a nearby mine. The CCC built a wooden lookout tower there in 1939. It was replaced with a fifty-three-foot steel tower in 1975. The lookout is staffed only during periods of high fire danger.

End:
Pactola Lake
44
385
BLACK HILLS
NATIONAL
FOREST
Start:
Sheridan Lake
Esri, NASA, NGA, USGS, South Dakota Department of Transportation

8.4 mi **Recommended Stop at Pactola Dam.**

Rapid Creek: Pactola Dam is fed by Rapid Creek, which includes water from North Rapid, Rapid, Slate, and Castle Creeks. Rapid Creek's headwaters begin near the Wyoming state line, flowing through the Black Hills and onto the plains where it meets the Cheyenne River about six miles east of Rapid City. It is one of the Black Hills' main drainages, along with Spearfish and Whitewood Creeks.

Humans along Rapid Creek: Rapid Creek has a long history of human occupation. Native peoples followed its course in and out of the Black Hills, as whites did later. For instance, John Brennan and a few other prospectors left their placer workings in Palmer Gulch and followed Rapid Creek out of the Black Hills. They established Rapid City along its course in February 1876. Settlements and activities along Rapid Creek have included mining camps, timber camps, health resorts, and vacation retreats.

Gold: Prospectors searched for gold along Rapid Creek in 1875, with at least ten men staking claims by 1876. While they found some gold, it was not in paying quantities (the amount needed to return more than a day's wages). Nevertheless, towns took root. Camp Crook, named in honor of the general, formed in the broad valley where Pactola Lake is today. Once the U.S. government annexed the Black Hills from the Great Sioux Reservation, the number of residents surged to 300. Despite the limited quantities of gold, the camp gained a hotel and a general store. A Deadwood-to-Custer wagon road also passed through the valley, providing trade for the businesses. The town faltered as most people moved on to Deadwood Gulch in 1876. When that excitement died down, the little camp came back to life, but the residents decided to change its name. Travelers had consistently confused it with Crook City, a town east of Deadwood. One man suggested Pactola, a reference to Pactolus, the Lydian river of golden sands, now known as Sart Çayı, on the Aegean coast of Turkey. According to myth, the legendary King Midas enriched the Pactolus with gold while bathing in its waters. Despite the optimistic name only limited quantities of gold were found near Pactola or along Rapid Creek.

George Alexander Grant's photo of the Musekamp residence in Silver City, before the construction of Pactola Dam inundated the area, 30 October 1948.
South Dakota State Historical Society

Rapid Canyon Railroad: Miners and merchants managed to keep Pactola alive over the years. A small boom came when the Rapid Canyon Line Railroad (RCL) built through in 1906. This little rail line has a long and convoluted history. It went by many names, but the RCL is probably the most descriptive. It began in 1886 when attorney William T. Coad conceived of building a railroad to the mines in the central Black Hills and turning Rapid City into a mining center. It took time for his idea to develop, but by 1891 he had decided to build his rail line from Rapid City to Mystic, up Rapid Canyon. Not only would this route reach the mines, but it would also connect with the newly constructed Burlington Railroad at Mystic. With the railroads exchanging freight and passengers, Coad forecast reduced transportation costs for Rapid City. As he raised money and started building his little line, he found the project much more expensive and difficult to complete than he envisioned. After thirteen years of struggle, he had only managed to build a few miles of track. He went broke in 1904, and the line sold at foreclosure. His primary contractor, C. D. Crouch, purchased it. Crouch managed to raise the money to finish the thirty-two-mile railroad, which included constructing over 100 bridges. What was now called the Crouch Line opened on 26 March 1906.

The Crouch Line seemed doomed from the start. A year after it opened, a flood washed out many of its bridges. After rebuilding, the company suffered several accidents, some of which resulted in fatalities and expensive litigation. Then the railroad failed to draw enough traffic to profit. It survived by hauling logs for the Warren-Lamb Lumber Co. and by transporting tourists, sightseers, fisher-people, and campers. As it struggled to make money, the owners threatened to abandon the line, but Rapid City businessmen, led by C. C. Warren and C. T. Lamb, saved it in 1920. World War II brought a small surge in traffic. The railroad carried troops out of Rapid City and hauled tank cars of fuel into town for the new Rapid City Army Air Base (now Ellsworth AFB). But the lack of wartime labor caused maintenance to be deferred, and the line deteriorated, leading to its abandonment in 1947.

Bernice Musekamp: The town's most famous resident was Bernice Musekamp. She opened a small store in Pactola to serve auto and rail travelers in 1926, but she altered her business over the years. In the 1930s, she added a dance hall and restaurant, and at one point she opened what was called Moose Camp Lodge or Moosecamp Park. It consisted of a restaurant, eleven cabins, an icehouse, and a hunting lodge.

Prohibition: The outlawing of alcohol in the 1920s brought moonshiners to the area. The remote location offered some advantages: the railroad brought in corn and other grains, the creek provided water, and the Black Hills offered plenty of hiding places. The proliferation of stills led to the area's nickname, "the valley of a thousand smokes." The illicit liquor reportedly brought interesting people to town, including Poker Alice Tubbs, who purchased supplies for her brothel in Sturgis.

Depression Era Gold Rush: Another minor boom developed when the federal government raised the price of gold during the Depression. Gold seekers prospected all along Rapid Creek. Some of their holes and waste piles are still evident, especially west of Pactola Lake.

The end of Pactola: When the Bureau of Reclamation started developing Pactola Dam in 1946, it brought an end to the little settlement. Musekamp and other landholders were forced to sell to the Bureau. Some of the buildings were relocated, the rest demolished. One structure went to the Hill City area and was eventually incorporated into the Prairie Berry Winery complex.

Damming Rapid Creek: Developers had envisioned building dams in the Rapid Creek drainage since settlers first arrived. The first significant effort came in 1890 when the Upper Rapid City Company built Canyon Lake Dam as part of a planned resort four miles above Rapid City.

During the Depression and drought of the 1930s, the Bureau of Reclamation built dams and irrigation districts across the West. Surveyors from the bureau examined Rapid Creek's drainage in 1937 and developed the Rapid Valley Project. It included money to build dams at Pactola and Deerfield (on Castle Creek), and to create an irrigation district of 12,000 acres in Rapid Valley. The Pactola portion, however, stalled because the irrigation users would have had to pay for relocating the railroad and highway that ran through the valley, making the project too expensive. Despite the setback, the government moved ahead with Deerfield Dam, completing it in 1946.

Pactola Dam: The Pactola project came back to life when the Missouri River flooded in the 1940s. This got the U.S. Army Corps of Engineers involved, the agency in charge of controlling flood waters and navigation. Both the Corps and the Bureau of Reclamation investigated the Missouri River drainage, looking for possible dam locations, but with different intentions. The Corps had flood control in mind, while the Bureau worried about irrigation. Each developed their own plan. Congress asked for a compromise, resulting in the Pick-Sloan Plan (Pick was with the Corps and Sloan with the Bureau). The resulting authorization became known as the Missouri River Basin Project of 1944. It called for the construction of six dams on the Missouri River, with four in South Dakota, to be managed by the Corps. Additional dams on the river's tributaries would be managed by the Bureau. After investigating Black Hills locations, the Bureau authorized Angostura Dam on the Cheyenne River in the southern Black Hills, and it reauthorized the Pactola project. When the railroad through Rapid Canyon closed in 1947, one major obstacle had been removed. Construction on Pactola Dam began in 1952 and was completed in 1956. The reservoir was designed to hold 99,000 acre feet of water (an acre foot is approximately 326,000 gallons), of which 43,000 acre feet were left empty for flood control storage. Conservation storage amounted to 55,000 acre feet and dead storage totaled 1,000 acre feet.

Rapid City Flood of 1972: The most significant flood to hit the Rapid Creek drainage was the Black Hills flood of 1972. A government study estimated that Pactola prevented $434,000 of losses in Rapid City—unfortunately, the city suffered over $100 million in damages. The heaviest rainfall was on the Black Hills' eastern slope, below the dam.

Dam modifications: A 1982 safety evaluation found that a "once in a century" flood would top the existing dam by six feet for approximately eight hours, causing it to fail and putting Rapid City underwater. The Bureau of Reclamation raised the dam fifteen feet and widened the spillway. Some skeptics have argued that the Bureau undertook the project to keep the agency busy after the federal government had ended the era of building big western dams.

Water allocation: The Bureau of Reclamation developed Pactola Dam and the Rapid Valley Project primarily for irrigation. Under a 1952 contract, irrigators controlled more than 60 percent of Pactola's water, or just over 34,000 acre feet per year. Ellsworth AFB and Rapid City were allocated about 26 percent, or 14,500 acre feet. The Bureau of Reclamation kept 6,000 acre feet for fish and wildlife conservation. When the original contract expired in 1992, the various entities began talks to reallocate the water. It took thirteen years, but in 2005, the city, the Rapid Valley Conservation District, and the Bureau of Reclamation finally agreed to turn over 89 percent of the lake's water, or 49,000 acre feet, to Rapid City. The Bureau retained the remainder. The irrigators agreed to the change with the understanding that they still had access to 8,000 acre feet in Deerfield Dam, and that they no longer had to cover the majority of Pactola's operating expenses. Although the city took over the costs, the Rapid City negotiators saw the agreement as the best way to guarantee a long-term water source. Ironically, the city gets most of its water from wells drilled into the Madison Aquifer because well water requires less treatment and costs less to supply than lake water.

Silver City: Located at the western tip of Pactola Lake, Silver City started out as Camp Gorman, named after the Gorman brothers. The three brothers reportedly developed two mines and uncovered some valuable ore in the area, but one died and the other two left before doing much with it. As reports of mineral-bearing rock spread, more people arrived and the camp became known as Silver City. It grew to about 300 people by 1878. Outside of a few mines in Sunnyside Gulch, north of town, the area yielded little wealth. Some residents blamed confusion over the type of metal, with reports mentioning everything from gold to antimony. Others claimed that the ore needed to be treated in a smelter. A bright future seemed assured when a smelter opened in Rapid City and the Rapid Canyon Line built through in the early twentieth century, but little ore was ever mined. Instead, the railroad primarily hauled logs to Warren-Lamb's sawmill in Rapid City. Today Silver City is home to a handful of full-time and part-time residents.

Silver City mineral exploration: The possibility of renewed mining just north of Silver City has become a concern in recent years. Since 2018, a Minneapolis exploration company known as F3 Gold has sought permission to drill forty-two test holes on federal and private land. Based on an updated geologic model, the company believes that an undiscovered gold deposit exists in the area. Under federal law, it has the right to drill on National Forest land, so long as it follows federal guidelines. The company has worked hard to win over nearby residents but has still met considerable resistance. Rapid City's Council voted against the project in early 2020. While F3 Gold continues to seek permission to drill, the Forest Service has been debating whether to withdraw the area from mineral location.

Placerville: Placerville is about one mile below Pactola Dam along the creek. Today it is the location of a United Church of Christ camp, but as the name implies, it once supported placer mining. The first major mining operation came when New York developer L. A. Richards founded the Bed Rock Gold Mining Company in 1902. He claimed to have a low-cost, high-volume placer machine that could profitably recover gold from Rapid Creek. Over the next eight years, Richards and another operator constructed a small dam at Pactola, built trestles and ditches for a three-mile flume, and installed hydraulic nozzles and sluicing equipment. The operation, however, failed to pay. Despite its poor showing, prospectors continued to explore the area, especially during the Depression, but Placerville never again received much attention.

Electrical generation: While Richards struggled with his gold operation, he became convinced that the volume and velocity of water in Rapid Creek could be used to generate electricity. By 1907, he started extending his flume to a location below Placerville where he envisioned building a hydroelectric plant, but his efforts came to naught. He ended up selling his water rights, ditch, and flume to Rapid City businessman George Mansfield, founder of the Dakota Power Company, which would eventually extend the flume farther down Rapid Creek to Big Bend.

Placerville Retreat: After the placer operations closed, Placerville's attractive setting and convenient location on the Rapid Canyon Line attracted picnickers and campers. The Congregational church has hosted summer camps there since 1920.

Johnson Siding: About a mile below Placerville is Johnson Siding. In 1892, a family of Swedish immigrants homesteaded on land

Rapid Creek, near Placerville, 2017. Note the remains of bridge supports for the Rapid Canyon Line. *Author photo*

around Rapid Creek and opened a sawmill, cutting timber from their own land and from neighboring parcels. It was generally a small operation, supplying local needs, but they sometimes handled large orders. During the construction of the railroad down Rapid Canyon, the Johnsons supplied ties and bridge timbers. Once the line opened in 1906, the railroad established a rail stop and siding near the sawmill, naming it "Johnson Siding." With better transportation, the Johnsons saw their market double. Another boost in business came when the Dakota Power Co. used Johnson lumber to extend L. A. Richards's flume to Big Bend, completing it in 1912. The Johnson family occasionally moved their sawmill to be closer to uncut timber, but they have been out of business for some time.

Big Bend: About two miles below Johnson Siding is Big Bend, named after a bend in Rapid Creek. Here Dakota Power opened its hydroelectric plant in 1912, but an inconsistent water supply interfered with operations. The water froze in the winter and disappeared during dry periods. Financial problems also dogged the company. Nevertheless, the plant operated until the company sold the equipment during World War II. Today the old hydro plant is a bed & breakfast.

Thunderhead Falls and Fort Meade Hydraulic Company: A tourist attraction called Thunderhead Falls once stood three and a half miles below Pactola Dam, around the corner from the power plant. It featured a 600-foot-long tunnel with a waterfall at the end. Today the attraction is closed, but water still flows through the tunnel. The Fort Meade Hydraulic Gold Mining Company, with Robert Flormann in charge, started the tunnel in the fall of 1879. The company's name reportedly came from officers at Fort Meade who had invested, but Flormann may have used it to give his operation creditability. In any case, Flormann's idea was to drain the creek at Big Bend by diverting the water through the tunnel, dig into the exposed creek bed, and uncover a fortune in gold-ladened gravel. He would then use the water rushing through his tunnel to recover the gold in a sluice box. The company closed by 1882 before the tunnel was finished. A local newspaper later scolded Flormann for squandering money on useless work. Without saying so, the paper, and many others, suspected Flormann of doing just enough work to keep his investors happy while he pocketed most of the money.

Big Bend Hydraulic Company: In 1883, a year after Fort Meade Hydraulic closed, the Big Bend Hydraulic Company was formed and followed a similar pattern. It promised to finish the tunnel, expose the creek, and sluice the gold out of the gravel. Over the next four years, the operatives declared at least thirty-eight dividends, paying out nearly $150,000 to investors, but the money did not come from gold production—it came from selling more and more stock, which was easy to do since the company was declaring dividends. Local people denounced it as a fraud, and T. H. White, a local mining engineer, de-

A section of the 600-foot tunnel started by the Fort Meade Hydraulic Company and later completed by the Big Bend Hydraulic Company, 1968.
South Dakota State Historical Society

cried the situation in an article in the *Engineering and Mining Journal.* Although the company sued White for libel, it was indeed a fraud, and the operators disappeared by 1889.

The upshot of these two operations was a 600-foot tunnel, which got close enough to the creek on the other side of the hill to punch a hole in the creek bed. Water flowed through the hole, creating a waterfall and a small stream in the tunnel. Other gold companies later worked this area but failed to find much gold.

Part Seven Galena
The Silver Camp

Route Overview: From Pactola Lake, travel north on US 385 to Galena Road. Turn right (east) onto Galena Road. Travel through Galena to Butcher Gulch Lane. Take Butcher Gulch Lane to Vinegar Hill Cemetery for a Recommended Stop.

Mileage starts at Pactola Lake.

0.0 mi **Pactola Lake: Return to US 385 and travel north.**

2.1 mi **Junction with SD 44:** Rimrock Highway, or SD 44, roughly parallels Rapid Creek as it flows to Rapid City. The road provides access to many of the historic locations in Rapid Canyon. The word "rimrock" refers to the cliffs that tower over the creek in several places.

6.4 mi **Trout Haven:** The remains of a former tourist attraction known as Trout Haven sit just off the road, near the intersection of US 385 and Rochford Road. It opened in the late 1950s, offering a no-hassle fishing experience. It was converted into a campground in recent years, perhaps reflecting the traveling public's changing views on how to spend vacation time and a declining interest in fishing.

11.0 mi **Experimental Forest Road:** The road to the west of US 385 leads to a 3,400-acre outdoor laboratory that opened in 1961. It is one of more than eighty Experimental Forests that the U.S. Forest Service established to study forest management techniques across the nation. The agency created the Black Hills Experimental Forest to study high-quality timber production and to determine how management philosophies affect other resources.

11.8 mi **Custer Peak Glimpses:** The distinctive peak seen in the distance on the trip north is Custer Peak, named by Captain William Ludlow,

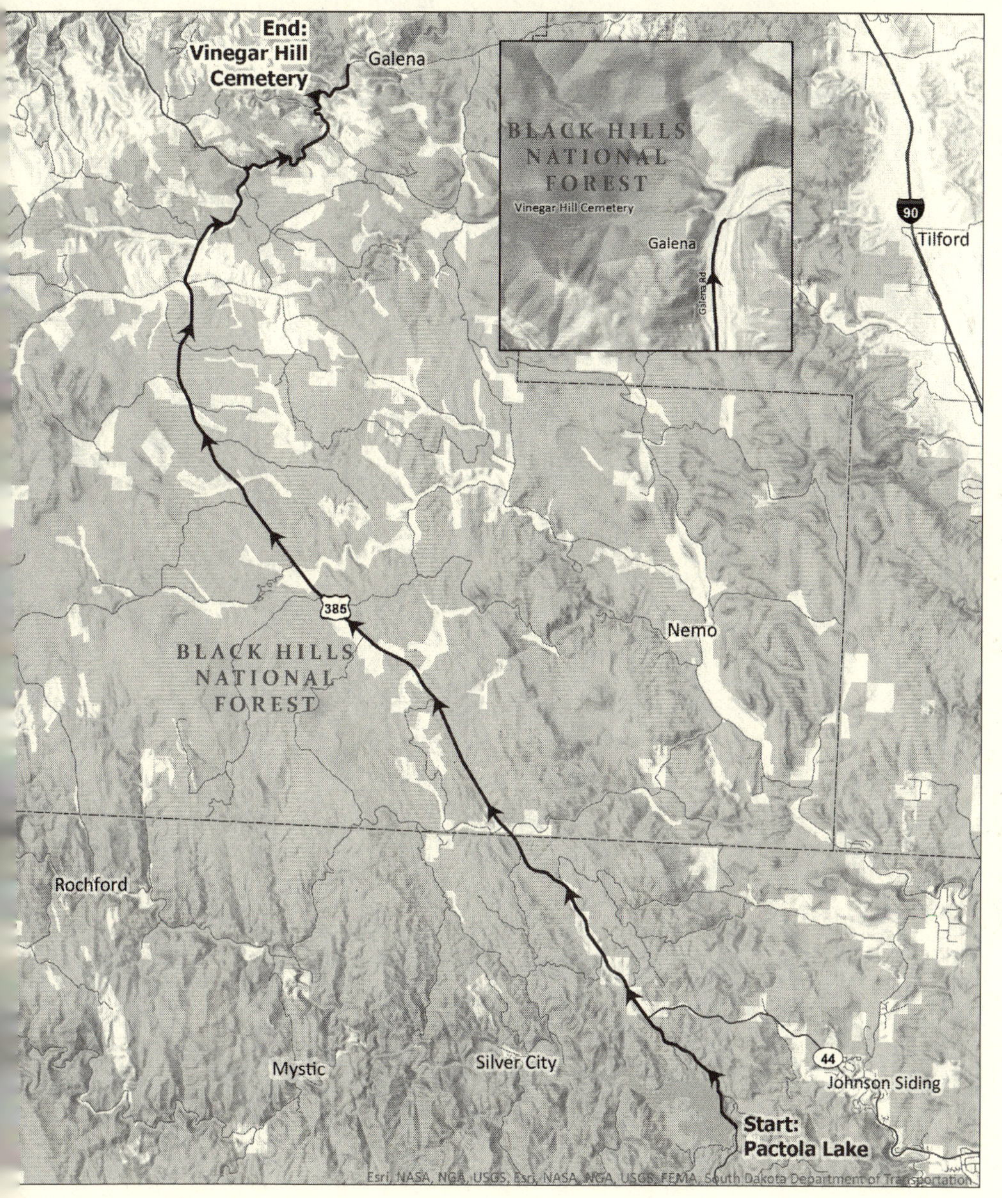
End:
Vinegar Hill
Cemetery
Galena
BLACK HILLS
NATIONAL
FOREST
Vinegar Hill Cemetery
Galena
Galena Rd
90
Tilford
385
Nemo
BLACK HILLS
NATIONAL
FOREST
Rochford
44
Johnson Siding
Mystic
Silver City
Start:
Pactola Lake
Esri, NASA, NGA, USGS, Esri, NASA, NGA, USGS, FEMA, South Dakota Department of Transportation

the chief of engineers for the Custer Expedition. At 6,794 feet, it is the tenth-highest summit in the Black Hills. The combination of location and elevation made it a good candidate for a fire lookout. The first was built in 1911 and the current lookout was built by the CCC in 1941. It was listed on the National Register of Historic Places in 1990.

12.7 mi **Mountain Meadows:** A small community known as Mountain Meadows sat in Middle Boxelder Creek Valley. It served area ranch families and travelers on the Deadwood trail. On the northern edge of the valley, just off Roubaix Lake Road, is Mountain Meadows cemetery.

Nasby: Black Hills maps occasionally show a small community called Nasby near Mountain Meadows. The earliest reference to Nasby in Black Hills newspapers is from 1895, and the town seems to have disappeared in the 1920s. Never very large, it apparently served area ranches with a post office, a school, and a few businesses. The origin of the unusual name is not known. It possibly came from a local family, or it could have been taken from a literary figure known as Petroleum V. Nasby, created by Ohio newspaperman David Ross Locke to satirize the South during the Civil War. Newspapers did refer to an outspoken politician as a "Nasby" for years after Locke's death in 1888, but it seems unlikely that the Nasby reference endured long enough to be applied to this location.

12.7 mi **Roubaix Lake Road:** Roubaix Lake and picnic area sits a short distance down Roubaix Lake Road. The CCC built a dam across the Middle Fork of Boxelder Creek and developed a picnic area. The Forest Service has since replaced the picnic facilities. The CCC also had a camp just north of the dam from 1933 to 1941. Evidence of the camp still exists, and a marker indicating its location sits just west of US 385. Besides creating Roubaix Lake, the CCC also thinned trees and undertook conservation projects. The lake was named after a small mining town a few miles away. A mine owner had come from Roubaix, France, and brought the name with him.

14.2 mi **North Fork Boxelder Creek/Custer Crossing/Custer Crossing Road:** This area is one of many locations where the tour crosses the Custer Expedition's trail. In August 1874, Custer's column was traveling north as it looked to exit the Black Hills and head home. The highway crosses the expedition's path in the North Boxelder Creek drainage, close to the location known as Custer Crossing today.

18.0 mi **Brownsville and the Elk Creek Drainage:** Brownsville was a logging camp founded in the early 1880s to supply wood to the Homestake Gold Mine in Lead. Brownsville and Elk Creek are discussed in the Northern Black Hills–Homestake tour.

18.8 mi **Rail Line to Galena:** The road named Old Ironhorse sits on the railroad bed of a branch line the Burlington Railroad built to Galena in 1902. The tour roughly follows the railroad bed to Galena.

20.6 mi **Galena Road, Turn to the right onto Galena Road.**
Bear Butte Creek: Galena Road follows Bear Butte Creek into Galena. This creek forms in the higher hills. After flowing through Galena, it heads east toward Sturgis but is generally dry as it exits the Black Hills. Like several other Black Hills creeks, its water disappears into a limestone layer and then reemerges later. Water reappears in Bear Butte Creek near Bear Butte Peak, the origin of the creek's name.

22.7 mi **Virginia City:** This town sat near the junction of Galena and Spring Run roads. It was also called Moll, after Samuel Moll, a past resident and one-time mayor of Galena. While the camp never grew beyond a few scattered cabins, it had one notable resident, Sarah ("Aunt Sally") Campbell, the African American cook who accompanied the 1874 Custer Expedition. She lived in Virginia City, working as a housekeeper and cook during the 1880s. She died there in 1888 and is buried in the Galena Cemetery.

Virginia City also marks the beginning of the Galena silver district. From near this location and extending through the town of Galena, miners opened a series of mines, with such names as the Comet, Horseshoe, Merritt, Silver Queen, Alice, Bion, and Rutherford B.

Hayes. The silver ore was found along two contacts or layers. A lower contact was close to the creek, and an upper contact was higher on the hill. Mine openings and waste piles can still be found along the hillsides, but tree growth has hidden most of the remains.

Prosperous mining towns in Nevada and Montana were also named "Virginia City," apparently reflecting the southern backgrounds of many of the miners. Those locations preceded the founding of this Black Hills camp. While it is unknown who brought the name to the Black Hills, it was probably used here by prospectors hoping to repeat the success of the Nevada and Montana mines.

23.3 mi **Strawberry Creek:** At this point the road crosses Strawberry Creek. There is also a Strawberry Ridge and a Strawberry Hill nearby. The inspiration for these names came from the area's wild strawberries. The closed road that parallels Strawberry Creek once went to the Gilt Edge Mine, which will be visited later in the tour. The road also passed the Union and Hoodoo Mines. These properties reportedly produced $150,000 of gold in the early twentieth century and would later become part of the Branch Mint Mining Company, also discussed later in the tour.

23.8 mi **Galena, Historic Mining Camp, 1875:** A roadside sign marks the beginning of the silver camp.

23.9 mi **Galena School:** On the left-hand (north) side of the road, slightly up the hill, is the Galena Schoolhouse. While classroom instruction started early in the camp's history, this schoolhouse was built in 1882 and used until 1943. Forty-one students were enrolled the year after it opened, and enrollment stayed around thirty-five for several years. The Galena Historical Society lovingly cares for the building, which is listed on the National Register of Historic Places.

24.0 mi **Downtown Galena:** A small white house is labeled "John Sheahan." He was a barber and used this structure for his business and home. The stone wall behind the building was part of the storeroom for the Dempsey saloon. As with all mining towns, Galena had an assortment of saloons, including the Corner Saloon, the Sudden Death Saloon,

The schoolhouse in Galena, 2022. *Author photo*

and Scandalous Bill's Joint. The town also had three hotels, including the American House and the Central House. Most of these were near this area.

24.1 mi **Historic Barn:** On the right-hand (south) side of the road, partially hidden by a modern home, is an historic barn, one of the few structures that remains from Galena's early days. It can often be seen in old photos of Galena.

24.1 mi **Custer Hill:** The mountain behind Galena, on the south and east, is traditionally known as Custer Hill. The waste pile from the Horseshoe-Comet Mine can barely be seen on its north slope, one hundred and fifty feet above the historic barn. Recent tree growth has largely hidden it. The Horseshoe-Comet produced silver in Galena's early years and pyrite for Deadwood's smelter in the 1890s. After operating intermittently, it closed in 1918.

24.3 mi **Walsh Cabin:** On the left (to the west), is a cabin associated with Thomas F. Walsh, perhaps Galena's most successful resident. After living here in 1877 and 1878, Walsh went to Colorado, where he be-

Thomas F. Walsh in 1904. *Library of Congress*

came wealthy at the Camp Bird Mine, outside of Ouray. With the wealth he earned, his daughter, Evalyn Walsh McLean, bought the Hope Diamond, a bluish-colored stone of more than forty-five carats, worth over $300 million today and now part of the Smithsonian Institution's collection. Although this structure looks more like a garage and is in poor condition, locals point to it as the Walsh cabin.

24.4 mi **Historic Structures:** On the left (west) are several buildings associated with the region's mining past. These served as businesses, houses, and boarding houses.

24.5 mi **Butcher Gulch Lane: At the intersection of Butcher Gulch Lane and Galena Road, turn onto Butcher Gulch Lane.**

24.5 mi **Borsch House:** The garage and house along Butcher Gulch Lane belong to descendants of the Borsch family. As Galena pioneers, the Borsch family ran saloons and boarding houses beginning in 1888. Fred Borsch III lived in this home until 1981. He became famous for owning Tootsie the Coyote, the official state animal. Tootsie is buried behind the house.

24.6 mi **Turn left (west) to Vinegar Hill Cemetery.**

24.8 mi **Vinegar Hill Cemetery: Recommended Stop.**
Like most mining camps, Galena's cemetery was built on a hill outside of town, away from valuable mineral land and far enough from camp to keep infectious diseases from spreading. The cemetery contains a representative example of Galena pioneers. Notable graves include:

Fred Borsch with Tootsie the Coyote, ca. 1950s. *South Dakota State Historical Society*

Fred Borsch & Tootsie: At one time, Fred Borsch owned a large amount of property in Galena as well as the Spot Liquor in Deadwood. His claim to fame was Tootsie the Coyote, his pet from 1947 to 1959. After the animal was found near Custer Peak, Borsch trained her to howl on command. In fact, Borsch discovered that Tootsie enjoyed chocolate. To get her to howl, he would break off a square from a Hershey's milk chocolate bar and set it in front of Tootsie. She would then throw back her head and howl. This talent made Tootsie famous, and Borsch willingly displayed her at his Deadwood store, in parades—including the Rose Bowl parade—and even on the Lawrence Welk Show. In 1949, the South Dakota legislature named Tootsie the official state animal.

Aunt Sally: After leaving the Black Hills with Custer, Sarah Campbell returned in 1876, working as a housekeeper and cook. She eventually moved in with a fellow she took care of, and they lived in a cabin near Virginia City until she died in 1888. In 1934, Galena residents placed a wooden sign on her grave to acknowledge her place in Black Hills history. When the Galena Historical Society recently installed a new headstone, the members used the same epitaph as had been on the original.

Pat Gorman: For a mining camp, Galena was not very violent, but a dispute between two mining companies, the Sitting Bull and the Richmond, resulted in one man's death. In the fall of 1882, Pat Gorman, one of the owners of the Richmond Mine, attacked Frank Davey, the son of the Sitting Bull Mine's owner, on the steps of the Galena post office. William Thatcher, a clerk for the Sitting Bull, quickly intervened, shooting and killing Gorman. Thatcher stood trial for murder but was found not guilty. Witnesses reported that Gorman started the fight and provoked the violence, with many adding that he was a disagreeable man, prone to violent outbursts.

Review of Galena's History:

Galena's founding: In 1875–1876, prospectors fanned out looking for precious metals. While gold was the metal of choice, they also looked for silver. Galena was one of the two locations in the Black Hills where prospectors identified significant silver deposits. The first claims were reportedly staked in 1875, starting with the Sitting Bull, and the town of Galena soon followed. Other camps, such as Cariboo and Hardscrabble, were quickly established nearby, but the entire area soon became known as Galena, after a type of silver ore which generally contains a large percentage of lead sulfide. This type of ore was found elsewhere in the country and fostered such towns as Galena, Illinois, and Galena, Missouri, both of which boomed primarily because of the ore's lead content. Black Hills prospectors hoped to succeed by producing silver.

Main economic supports: The best mines, including the Florence, the Sitting Bull, and the Richmond, sat at the lower, east end of town.

Galena in 1877. *Deadwood History, Inc.*

Small smelters were built nearby, the first in 1879. Most proved inefficient and operated intermittently, leaving little indication of where they stood.

Galena went through the boom-and-bust cycles typical of mining camps. Despite hopes of a great silver find, most mines were not very rich. While some surface assays brought spectacular results, these deposits had been concentrated over the eons, and after a little depth, the ore carried much less silver. The mines sat undeveloped and the camp remained small, counting only about sixty people in the early years. Better days came when the Sitting Bull expanded operations in 1880, with Galena hitting a high point of 400 people and seventy-five structures. After the Sitting Bull closed in the 1890s, other mines opened, including nearby gold mines, and the town stabilized. The 1890 census counted 252 residents, and the 1900 tally found 251. Mining ground to a halt in the early twentieth century, leaving the town nearly deserted by 1920.

Value of silver: Besides marginal quantities of ore, the depressed price for silver also hurt production. Gold has always been valued more highly. In the early 1870s, a prospector could get $20 for an ounce of gold, but only around $1.25 for the same amount of silver. Even so, silver could still be produced at a profit, allowing mines in Nevada and Colorado to flourish. The situation changed in 1873, just before the Black Hills discoveries. In that year, the U.S. government adopted the gold standard, and countries that had used silver as the medium of exchange in their colonies, such as England and Germany, followed suit. These changes caused the price of silver to drop dramatically. Under pressure from western silver miners, Congress passed measures mandating that the government buy silver to boost its price. These actions brought little relief, and the price of silver continued to fall, declining to seventy-eight cents per ounce by 1893.

Richmond–Sitting Bull fight: Despite the limited incentive to mine silver, two mines that sat next to each other on Custer Hill had enough value to operate: the Richmond and the Sitting Bull. The Sitting Bull in particular brought a small boom to Galena from 1881 to 1883. Colonel John Davey, described as a Chicago capitalist, came to the Black Hills in 1877. He arrived in Galena and purchased the Florence and the Sitting Bull in 1880. He fired up a thirty-ton smelter and soon produced $410,000 in silver. This activity caused Galena's population to hit 400. The Davey smelter left a slag pile that is still visible.

Davey disputed the location of the silver vein with the owner of the neighboring Richmond Mine. Each side claimed that it was on his property. It was during this dispute that William Thatcher killed Pat Gorman in downtown Galena. After that violent outburst, the Richmond–Sitting Bull fight went into litigation in 1883. While the court case proceeded, the Richmond owners brought an injunction against Davey, forcing him to stop work and costing 125 men their jobs. As the case dragged on, Davey ran out of money and sold the Sitting Bull in 1889. Despite the legal dispute, the new owner reopened the mine and produced $41,000 in silver from 1889 to 1891. The court case went on for sixteen years, and besides nearly killing Galena's best mine, it highlighted a weakness in the nation's mining laws: under the 1872

Mining Law, a mine owner could follow a vein from its surface apex to wherever it leads, with the assumption that it plunges into the earth. The Galena ore bodies, however, are flat, without a clearly defined apex. Because of this court case, a new understanding of mineral veins resulted, which took into account flat formations.

Because of their value, the Richmond and Sitting Bull Mines caught the attention of investors when the Depression hit. In 1930–1931, DeWolfe Barton gained control of the two mines and built a flotation processing plant. Poor returns forced him to close after only six months. The plant was dismantled in 1945. In the 1960s, the properties, renamed the Double Rainbow, again attracted attention when the price of silver increased from $8 per ounce in 1960 to $18 per ounce in 1968. Newmont Exploration, the National Science Foundation, the U.S. Geological Survey, and the Homestake all showed interest. In 1967, the Homestake sank a shaft and did some exploration. While it encountered some good ore pockets, the company found too little silver to merit mining. Remnants of the flotation plant and the Homestake head frame can still be seen near Bear Butte Creek below Galena.

Railroad construction: Even without any significant silver production, the Burlington built a branch line into Galena in 1902. Harris Franklin had persuaded the railroad's managers that a rail connection would allow him to reopen mines and ship Galena ore to his Deadwood smelter. But this hope proved illusory. While the Burlington shipped some ore, the smelter could not treat it profitably and soon closed. The rail branch lasted for about twenty years, carrying little freight and losing money for the Burlington.

Branch Mint: Soon after the Burlington built into Galena, the town saw another hope for prosperity. Black Hills promoter James D. Hardin organized the Branch Mint Mining Company and gained control of over 200 claims, or about 1,800 acres, becoming the area's largest claim holder in 1903. His property included the Hoodoo and Union Hill Mines, which had already produced $150,000 of gold. Hardin also announced plans to build a large stamp mill, a cyanide plant, and a three-mile-long railroad to connect the mines to the mill in lower Galena. He wanted to have his new company producing gold by 1 June 1904.

Despite his ambitious timeline, it took Hardin until November 1907 to start production, and by then the company was buried in debt. Creditors and workers wanted to be paid, while investors demanded returns on the hundreds of thousands of dollars they had spent. After operating for only a few months, Hardin stepped away and leased the company to New York financiers. These men attempted to pay off debts and set the Branch Mint on the right path, but the problems were too great. Hardin got the operation back in 1909, but it remained idle and went into receivership. When the property went up for sale at a sheriff's auction in 1913, Hardin made one last attempt to regain control, but with no luck. The equipment was eventually sold, and no credible production figures can be found. The high hopes Galena residents had for another boom failed to materialize, and the town's population dropped to 109 by 1910.

Hardin's intent is a mystery. By the time he developed the Branch Mint, he had become a well-known promoter and speculator. His family had arrived in the Two Bit Creek area, a few miles north of Galena, in 1877. Over the next several years he attempted to turn idle claims into paying mines, but with little luck. Hardin then acquired a large piece of land along the Redwater River between Spearfish and Belle Fourche to build a hydroelectric plant, hoping to power an electric rail line he envisioned developing through the northern Black Hills. It was after that project stalled that he became interested in the Branch Mint.

The size of the Branch Mint operation, from the mill to the railroad, would seem to indicate that it was an investment scam. Large undertakings and expensive improvements were often done to impress investors. While Hardin sold stock in the East, he never fled the Black Hills, as often happened in investment schemes. He instead seems to have simply been a promoter with big ideas. At one time or another he represented eight companies, serving as general manager for each one. None of them made money, at least for the investors, and maybe not for Hardin. He died where he began, on Two Bit Creek, apparently destitute. He and his wife are buried there.

Lee Russell's photo of James and Nellie Hardin, 1937.
South Dakota State Historical Society

Galena's survival: Galena survives today with a mix of full-time and part-time residents. It has also become a mecca for Black Hills visitors, but for different reasons than Deadwood. Tourists visit that Wild West town to find Wild Bill and Calamity Jane. Galena lacks such famous personalities. Instead, a number of off-road trails converge on Galena Road, and the town can get quite busy with people buzzing through on their ATV/UTVs.

Part Eight The Gilt Edge Mine

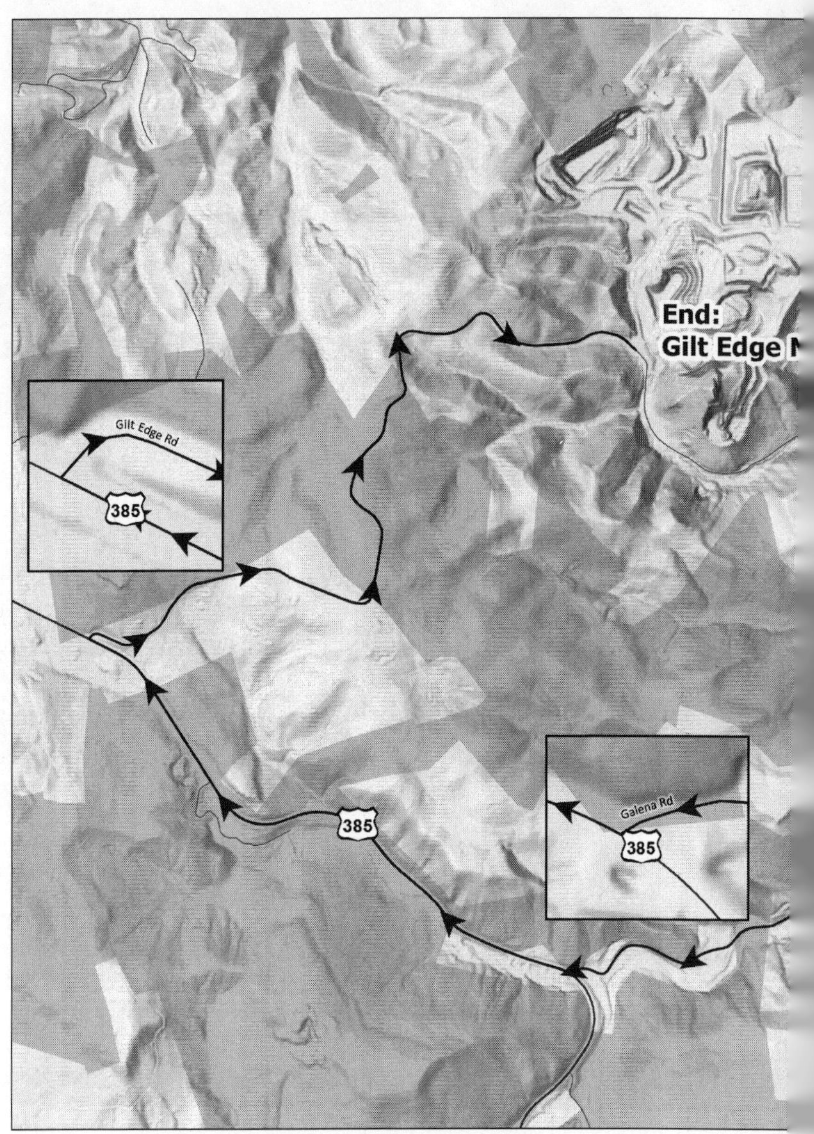

Route Overview: From Galena Cemetery, travel east through lower Galena. Then turn around to take Galena Road to US 385. Turn right (north) onto US 385. At Gilt Edge Road, turn right and travel to the open pit mine for a Recommended Stop.

Mileage starts at Galena Cemetery.

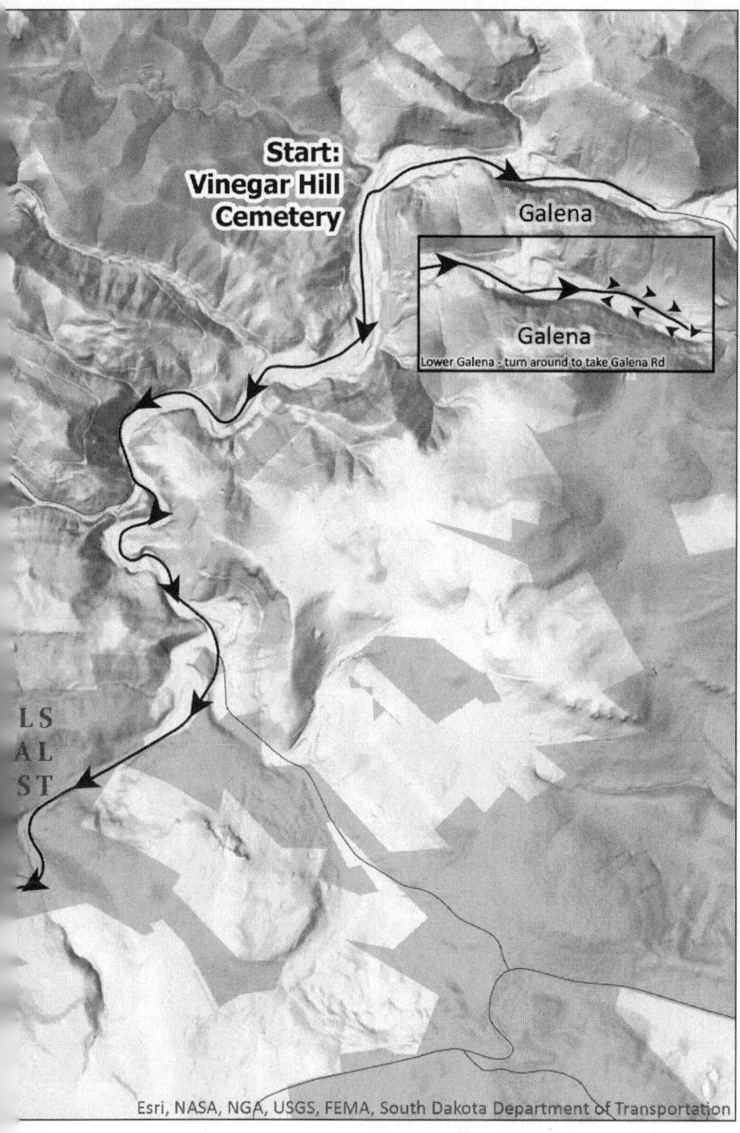

0.0 mi **Galena Cemetery: Return to Butcher Gulch Lane.**

0.2 mi **Intersection of the road to the cemetery and Butcher Gulch Lane: Turn right (south) toward Galena Road.**

"China Walls": A popular ATV/UTV trail goes up the hill to the left. It passes a series of rock walls that have become popularly known as the "China Walls." The walls were built as part of a development scheme involving the Hercules Mine. Prospectors located the Hercules claim as early as 1887, hoping to find gold, but there was none. In 1908, the owners announced that they had uncovered a large ledge of copper and planned to build a mill. Construction began in 1909, but all that was accomplished was the completion of the mill's foundation, the rock walls. Passing years have erased the identities of those who built the walls, and it has become commonplace to assume Chinese craftsmen did it. But by 1909 there were few Chinese left in the Black Hills, and so it is unlikely that Chinese workers were responsible.

The "China" walls in Galena, once part of the Hercules claim and built around 1909. *Author photo*

The Branch Mint Stamp Mill and Cyanide Plant, ca. 1907. This photo was included in a company promotional poster.

0.3 mi **Galena Road. From Butcher Gulch Lane turn left (east) onto Galena Road.**

0.6 mi **Davey Smelter:** The road crosses the slag pile made by the Davey smelter. The smelter sat just to the right (south) of the road. It treated ore from the Sitting Bull Mine, which sat high on the hill behind the smelter. A small sign tacked to a tree reads, "Davey Smelter."

0.7 mi **Branch Mint Mill:** The earthen embankment to the left (north) was the location of Jim Hardin's Branch Mint mill. A new building sits on the mill's location. A stone wall from the mill is evident on the hillside behind the embankment.

Four-wheel drive option: People with high clearance or 4WD vehicles may wish to continue about a half mile down the road to the area of DeWolfe Barton's 1930–1931 processing plant and the Homestake's 1967 exploration shaft, on the opposite side of the creek. Not much remains and the road is rough. For those who wish to pursue it, this side trip is not included in the mileage calculation.

The Tour turns around in front of the Branch Mint location and returns to US 385.

5.2 mi **Galena Road ends at US 385: Turn right (north) onto US 385.**

6.7 mi **Junction of US 385 and Gilt Edge Road: Turn right (east) onto Gilt Edge Road. Travel to the end of the road.**

8.2 mi **Last Chance Ridge Road:** Two inaccessible historic sites are on Last Chance Ridge Road.

Golden Crest Mine: The Golden Crest Mine was reportedly located in 1876, but little happened with it until the 1890s. It then went through several ownership changes and was mined on and off for many years. In the process, it gained a hoist house, a stamp mill, a cyanide plant, a mine office, and a mine manager's house. The Commonwealth Company purchased the property in 1947 and modernized the plant in 1951, becoming the last company to operate it. One report claims that about $100,000 of gold was produced in the early days, but operating costs undoubtedly limited profits. In fact, some of

The Golden Crest Mine, by Lyndle Dunn.
E.Y. Berry Library, Black Hills State University

Remains of the Anchor Mountain Mine's arrastra, near Galena, 2011.
Author photo

the owners may have been more concerned about attracting investors than producing gold. The large complex of buildings stood until a 1972 fire destroyed several of them, leaving only the office, the manager's house, and piles of iron where the stamp mill once stood. The remaining buildings and most of the equipment have disappeared since then. It once was an interesting place to visit, but the current owner has closed it off. The mine's hoist is now displayed in front of the Sanford Visitor Center in Lead. It was moved there several years ago and painted blue.

Arrastra: Some distance down a branch of Last Chance Ridge Road is a stone and concrete basin set into the forest floor. Known as an arrastra (from the Spanish *arrastrar*, to drag along the ground), this device was used to crush ore. It has a rock floor, surrounded by a circular rock wall. At one time, a pole with arms stood in the center, and drag stones were suspended from the arms. The stones crushed the gold ore as horse, water, or some other power source rotated the center pole. Arrastras were crude, but fairly effective in crushing ore and releasing gold. This arrastra is believed to have been part of the Anchor Mountain Mine. It had ore similar to the neighboring Gilt Edge Mine, but no production records exist.

8.8 mi **Gilt Edge Mine, Recommended Stop.**

The large open pit was the site of the Gilt Edge Mine, which was reportedly located in 1876. Its name came from the belief that it sat on the edge of a gold mining area, much like the gilded pages of a book. Another meaning, however, may be appropriate today. "Gilded" refers to a golden covering hiding something worthless. In this case, the claim looked golden, but ended up causing big problems. Difficult ore prevented miners from recovering much gold in the early days. The mine owners tried treating the ore with the newly developed cyanide process in 1893, but it took until 1900 to figure out how to use the process effectively. With this success the mine operated until 1916 and again in the 1930s, producing over 57,000 ounces of gold and 25,000 ounces of silver. During its years of operation, the mill created a large sand pile that spread across the mine site.

In 1986, a Canadian-based company known as Brohm Mining acquired the Gilt Edge Mine and worked it through an open pit until the price of gold dropped in 1997. The company went bankrupt in 1999. Under Brohm's control, the Gilt Edge produced over 189,000 ounces of gold and 255,000 ounces of silver. The large sand pile also disappeared.

Upon bankruptcy, the company abandoned the 360-acre site, including the 265-acre open pit and a 60-acre waste rock dump. Unfortunately, the mine had encountered highly sulfuric ore, which turns rainwater acidic. The resulting environmental problems forced the Environmental Protection Agency (EPA) to declare it a superfund site in 2000, meaning a site that is contaminated by hazardous waste. The government sued the responsible parties, gaining $40 million, which it spent on reclamation, along with another $80 million of federal dollars. South Dakota also spent over $7 million. Since the initial cleanup, the federal government has paid 90 percent of the costs, the state 10 percent. It will take at least another $80 million to consolidate and cap the toxic waste. Once cleanup is complete, the state will be responsible for all operation and maintenance costs in perpetuity, unless a better solution can be found. About 95 million gallons of water are treated a year, which is dumped into Strawberry Creek. The state has recently taken control of the site, hoping to ensure that it will never again become a superfund site. In 2018, Agnico Eagle Mines of Toronto began exploring the site. The company claims that if paying quantities of gold are found, it can recover the gold while cleaning up the site more effectively than the state or federal governments.

Other claims: The Gilt Edge was just one of several claims in the area. Other mines included the Oro Fino, the Rattlesnake Jack, the Dakota Maid, the Two Bears, and the Anchor Hill. Mining companies thought these claims showed promise in the 1890s and 1900s, especially since the ore could be treated in Deadwood's smelter. The companies even convinced the Burlington to build a branch line into the area. The mines, however, produced little of value.

Part Nine The Gold Rush in Deadwood Gulch

Route Overview: Follow Gilt Edge Road to US 385. Turn right (north) onto US 385 and travel to its intersection with US 85. Turn right (east) toward Deadwood. Follow US 85 through Deadwood to the Rodeo Grounds. Turn right (south) into the Days of '76 Event Complex & Rodeo Grounds for a Recommended Stop.

Mileage starts at Gilt Edge Mine.

0.0 mi **Gilt Edge Mine: Follow Gilt Edge Road to US 385.**

2.0 mi **Junction of Gilt Edge Road and US 385: Turn right (north).**

2.3 mi **Strawberry Hill:** US 385 goes over what is known as Strawberry Hill. The highway over Strawberry Hill got its start as an early trail. Although several trails entered Deadwood, this one became the preferred route for north-south auto travel by 1914. In that year, the Lawrence County commissioners graded the first five miles up Strawberry Hill of what was called the "Deadwood-Denver Road" or the "Diamond D Hiway." It took over a decade, however, to make the entire road from Deadwood to Hot Springs suitable for auto travel.

4.7 mi **View of Yates Headframe:** The trip north on US 385 provides a view of the Yates headframe. The Yates and its sister headframe, the Ross, are area landmarks. The Homestake Mining Company dug two shafts and built the headframes during the 1930s. The shafts extend to a depth of over 5,000 feet. Sanford Laboratory now controls the shafts and has recently refurbished them to support its underground science experiments.

5.7 mi **Intersection of US 385 and US 85:**
Turn right (east) and follow US 85 through Deadwood to the Event Complex & Rodeo Grounds.

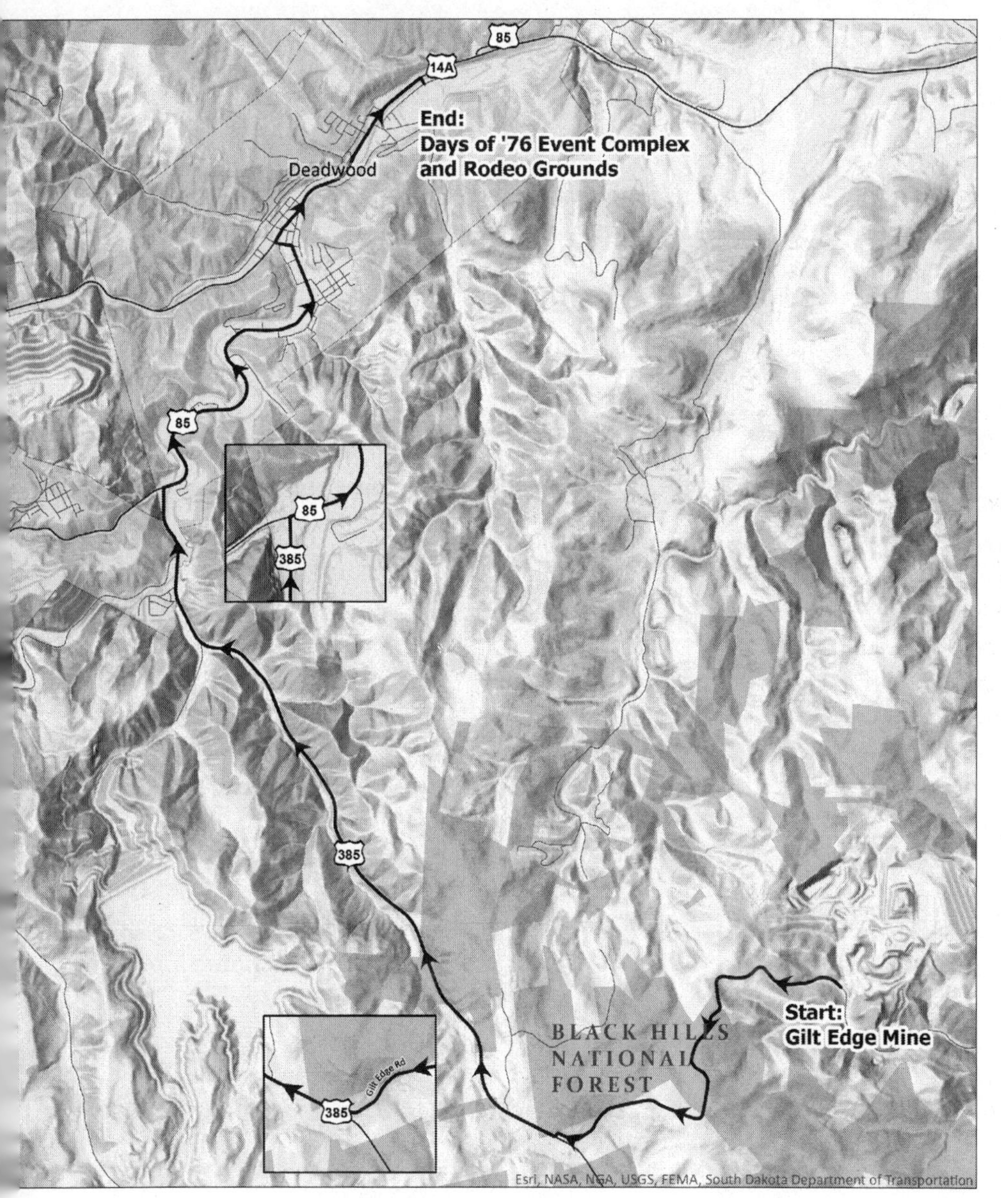
85
14A
End:
Days of '76 Event Complex
and Rodeo Grounds
Deadwood
85
85
385
385
BLACK HILLS
NATIONAL
FOREST
Start:
Gilt Edge Mine
Gilt Edge Rd
385
Esri, NASA, NGA, USGS, FEMA, South Dakota Department of Transportation

Deadwood: Only a few items relating to Deadwood's history are mentioned in this tour. The town's history is more fully covered in the Spearfish–Deadwood–Lead Tour.

5.8 mi **Pluma:** Near the intersection of US 385 and US 85 is the small town of Pluma. Since it sits at the confluence of Gold Run and Whitewood Creeks, and both creeks carried small quantities of gold, prospectors visited the area during the earliest days of the gold rush. But Pluma was not among the many camps that formed during those heady times. Instead, it came later, developing more as an outpost to the activities that went on in Lead and Deadwood.

Nevertheless, much happened over the years. The Custer-to-Deadwood Trail followed Whitewood Creek, bringing travelers through the Pluma area from 1876 until about 1890. In the earliest days, stagecoaches from Cheyenne used the route, and the first attempted robbery of a Black Hills stage happened near here. On 25 March 1877, gunmen stopped a northbound stage driven by Johnny Slaughter. During the holdup a man named Reddy fired a shotgun, killing Slaughter and causing the horses to bolt toward Deadwood. The outlaws fled, with a posse in hot pursuit. Despite their efforts, the outlaws remained at large. Sheriff Seth Bullock stayed on the case and eventually tracked Reddy to an Ohio jail. Despite Bullock's efforts, Reddy never stood trial for the killing of Johnny Slaughter.

Pluma did not yet exist at the time of this excitement, but three prospectors had already staked the "Pluma lode" on a hill east of the Homestake vein in June 1876. How they chose the name is unknown, but it could be a corruption of the Spanish word *plumas*, meaning feathers, which was used in California's gold country. Some of California's earliest finds came along the Feather River, called Rio de las Plumas by Spanish speakers. The reference to Plumas stuck and a California county carries that name today. With miners often naming their claims after successful mineral locations found elsewhere, these Black Hills men may have chosen Pluma to harken back to California's golden past. In any case, little happened with the Pluma lode until 1888, when the owners organized the Pluma Consolidated Gold Mining Company and brought in a twenty-stamp mill. They placed it on Whitewood Creek, just above its confluence with Gold Run Creek.

The opening of the "Pluma Mill" gave the entire location the name Pluma. When the Burlington Railroad opened a station here in 1890, company officials called it Pluma, ensuring the name's permanence.

Railroad connections brought more activity. Burlington trains running between Deadwood and Edgemont stopped at Pluma to exchange passengers and freight with Deadwood Central interurban trains that ran between Deadwood and Lead. The railroad also attracted patrons from outlying camps, such as Galena, and industries soon followed. The Belt Power & Light Company, taking advantage of the rail connections, built a power plant here in 1893. Though the plant was designed to provide electricity to Lead, the company wanted ready access to coal shipments. In 1895, the Horseshoe Mining Company opened a large chlorination plant, the Kildonan, next to the power plant, counting on rail transport to supply ore. These industries made Pluma a booming community by 1900, with a post office and a school district of over 140 students.

Pluma's population dwindled with the closing of the Kildonan mill and the transition from rail to auto travel. The school district counted only fifty students in 1920. The little town became a highway

The Belt Power and Light Company's plant in Pluma, ca. 1911.
South Dakota State Historical Society

The Kildonan gold mill in Pluma. *South Dakota State Historical Society*

crossroads, with new businesses opening, including a drive-in diner, a gas station, and motels. Over the years, these businesses have also disappeared. The last motel burned in the early 2000s. Pluma's roadside park sits on its location.

The City of Deadwood annexed Pluma in 1985. Still, hints of Pluma's past can be found. Chubby Chipmunk Hand-Dipped Chocolates has taken over the old gas station, electric transformers mark the location of the Belt electric plant, and a stone wall behind Chubby Chipmunk is from the Kildonan gold mill.

6.1 mi **Deadwood Gas Plant:** The area from Pluma into Deadwood was once home to several small industries, including a pole plant, a brickyard, and a gas plant. The Lead-Deadwood Gas and Fuel Company's gas manufacturing plant sat across from the Thunder Cove Lodge on US 85. Deadwood residents knew the advantages of using gas for lighting, cooking, and heating from the time of the town's founding, but they did not have natural gas in mind. Instead, they envisioned a gas manufactured by coal gasification, a technology widely used at the time. In the hopes of getting a plant, community leaders granted James McPherson a franchise in 1878, but nothing came of it. Another developer stepped forward and put in a gas system in 1894. It failed to live up to expectations. Finally, in 1904 the Lead-Deadwood Gas and Fuel Company built a plant along Whitewood Creek and laid gas lines throughout town. Although electricity had become available, some people preferred lighting with a gas flame, partly because the electric light bulb had yet to be fully refined. Nevertheless, the Burlington brought in coal, which was heated under pressure to release gas. Filtering through a water bath refined the gas. The finished product was then piped to a number of Deadwood locations, including the Franklin residence, today's Adams House. Several impurities remained in the gas, however, and over time they took a toll on the pipes, forcing the operation to close by the mid-1920s. The plant's ruins, including a large metal tank, sat along the highway into the 1980s.

7.1 mi **Burlington Railroad Yard:** The two-story wooden bank building at the corner of Sherman and Charles Streets once served as the Burlington Railroad's freight station. The building was moved a few hundred feet from its original location. Not far from the bank is a large shed that was once the Burlington's engine house, built to service the large mallet steam engines that ran between Edgemont and Deadwood. Once diesels replaced steam engines, the engine house primarily stored the Deadwood switch engine. The Sherman Street parking lot occupies the remainder of the Burlington's rail yards. It once contained several tracks, a small roundhouse, and a turntable. The Burlington quit running trains into Deadwood in 1983, and while it removed most of its tracks, the City of Deadwood purchased the line to Lead, hoping to open a tourist railroad. One operator took on the task from 1988 to 1990 but failed to profit. The tracks remain, now buried under sand and asphalt to accommodate the Mickelson Trail.

7.2 mi **Homestake Adams Research and Cultural Center (HARCC), 150 Sherman Street:** The modern building that shares the Sherman Street parking lot with the bank serves as the archives and administrative center for Deadwood History Inc. (DHI) and the Adams Museum & House. Black Hills jewelry company F. L. Thorpe built the structure to replace its Main Street headquarters, which burned in the 1987 Syndicate Block fire. The relocated business, however, did not last long. A worker strike and a competitive jewelry market convinced the owners to sell their business and building. When the Homestake Mining Co. donated its records to the Adams Museum, the city bought the structure, and the museum raised money to turn it into the archives. The HARCC opened in 2011.

7.4 mi **Adams Museum, 54 Sherman Street:** William Emery Adams, one of Deadwood's most successful grocers, built the Adams Museum and gave it to the city to honor Black Hills pioneers and his deceased first wife and two daughters in 1930. Although it is diminutive, the museum offers a good overview of Deadwood's past. The multi-story brick buildings across Sherman Street from the museum housed Adams's grocery warehouses.

7.5 mi **Intersection with Pioneer Way:**
Sherman Street meets Pioneer Way, US 85, at an angle. Turn right onto Pioneer Way and travel east to the Event Complex and Rodeo Grounds.

8.4 mi **Intersection of Pioneer Way with 76th Drive:**
The rodeo grounds are on the right (south). Turn in where the Days of '76 Museum sign points the way.

8.4 mi **First discovery historical marker:** The interpretative sign gives the details of the discovery of gold, but to summarize: Frank Bryant, John Pearson, and others came down Spruce Gulch and stopped on Whitewood Creek to check for gold in August 1875. After some digging, they grew discouraged and left. The gold was there; they had apparently set their sluice box at the wrong angle and failed to catch any. The men returned later in the year to renew the search. Despite their initial failure, they would later claim the first discovery of gold. Because of the circumstances involved in this event, it may be more accurate to state that the first discovery of gold actually happened just below Central City, near the confluence of Blacktail and Deadwood Creeks, in November 1875.

Recommended stop in lower Deadwood: Find a convenient location to stop. For a good view of the area, take the road to the left and go around the campground. Stop just past the South Dakota Highway Department facility or just before the Lead-Deadwood Sanitary District's property.

Early trails and settlements: Once gold was discovered, a number of trails dropped into Deadwood Gulch near this area. Routes from Custer either came through what was called Splittail Gulch, just to the east of here, or along the hillside next to Spruce Gulch, just to the south. The route from Crook City, a town northeast of Deadwood, also came into this part of town, sometimes using a trail that went behind the First Gold Hotel and at other times coming down the hill that carries US 85 today. Navigating the steep hills into the gulch generally required teamsters to tie ropes to their wagons and then ease them down the hill with the aid of stubbing posts.

Town creation: A series of towns also developed along Whitewood Creek. Montana City took root just below this location on Whitewood Creek; Fountain City popped up near where Cadillac Jack's casino is today; Elizabethtown formed a little farther up the gulch; and, of course, Deadwood came next. Each of these gained some population and a few businesses.

As different social classes arrived in the gulch, they generally settled in distinct sections. The majority of African Americans lived close to this area, while Chinese residents set up their homes and businesses closer to downtown Deadwood. But these separations were not emphatic. People of different ethnic and racial backgrounds could be found living throughout the gulch.

Gold mills: When the city of Deadwood was incorporated in 1881, this area became known as the First Ward, but its importance to the town really started when several gold mills opened in the late 1880s. In 1888, Deadwood businessmen built the Deadwood Reduction Works to treat ores from the Bald Mountain and Ruby Basin Mining Districts. It sat where the waste treatment plant is today. After it burned on 1 March 1889, two groups of entrepreneurs established plants to replace it. One group, led by James K. P. Miller, built a smelter. Their first plant was a small, experimental setup that they called the Baby Smelter. Built in 1889, it probably sat just about where the bridge over Whitewood Creek on US 14A is today. As they expanded the smelter, they moved it across the creek and named it the Deadwood & Delaware (D&D) Smelter. It produced $11 million in gold before closing in 1902, leaving behind the large slag pile that still exists below this location.

Harris Franklin led the other group. They had organized the Golden Reward Mining Company as the Reduction Works went up, and after the plant burned, they built a new one on its foundations, using the chlorination process for gold recovery. They successfully operated the plant until it was destroyed by a fire in 1899. The Golden Reward then built a cyanide plant at the same location in 1901. It ran until 1918. The stone foundations from these plants still stand behind the waste treatment facility. The ore for these gold mills primarily came from the Ruby Basin Mining District, west of Lead, bringing new life to a region that had produced little gold prior to their opening. Other

Smelters, cyanide plants, and railroads in lower Deadwood, ca. 1901.
Black Hills Mining Museum

The Fremont, Elkhorn and Missouri Valley Railroad's narrow gauge train near Deadwood. *South Dakota State Historical Society*

companies tried to imitate this success and established plants in the area, including the Consolidated, the Dakota, and the Imperial. Either because of poor management or poor-quality ore, these mills only worked intermittently before closing. The Days of '76 Museum partially sits on the site of the Imperial mill.

Industrial area: The gold mills added an industrial component to Deadwood, boosting the town's economy. They were built in this area because it had the room. Deadwood was located closer to the richest placer deposits, leaving this area lightly settled. Whitewood Creek had also created a flood basin in this area, discouraging development. The gold mills were set back from the creek and built on slightly elevated pieces of land to avoid any flooding.

Railroads: The Fremont, Elkhorn & Missouri Valley Railroad (Elkhorn) yards also sat in this area, opposite the gold mills. The railroad had a small roundhouse, a freight station, and sidings. The Elkhorn arrived in Deadwood in late 1890. It had built from Nebraska to Buffalo Gap in 1885, to Rapid City in 1886, and to Whitewood in 1887.

It then used Whitewood as the end of track for three years, much to the dismay of Deadwood's residents, who wanted a rail connection. When the railroad finally reached town on 29 December 1890, a grand celebration erupted. Thousands of people greeted the first train, followed by a parade and celebratory banquet. The Elkhorn then built a narrow gauge line through Deadwood to connect the Bald Mountain and Ruby Basin Mining Districts with the gold mills. After the gold mills closed, the narrow gauge tracks were abandoned by 1920. The standard gauge line that connected Whitewood to Deadwood lasted until 1967.

When the Burlington Railroad arrived in Deadwood in early 1891, it built through town to also reach this area's gold mills. Its tracks ran along the hillside to the south.

Days of '76 celebration: As the town's economy began to slip after the last of the gold mills closed, town leaders knew they needed to do something to help Deadwood recover. The moment of decision came when Lead broke an agreement to cohost a Fourth of July celebration in 1923. Realizing that their town was the only one in the Black Hills without a holiday event, members of the Deadwood Business Club decided to develop their own activity for 1924. To make it distinctive, they called it a "Days of '76 Homecoming celebration." The pageant would highlight the town's colorful past with a parade, reenactments of historic events, and appearances of famous characters—essentially a local version of Buffalo Bill's Wild West show. Backers organized a two-day event that included a parade, American Indian dances, shooting contests, bronco riding, horse races, mining demonstrations, trick riding, and a rodeo. At night, public dancing and band concerts were the fare. To make the town appealing to visitors, the planners encouraged local men to stop shaving, dress western, and put log fronts on their businesses. Reenactors played Wild Bill, Calamity Jane, and Preacher Smith. The event also featured a highly romanticized version of the trial of Wild Bill's killer, Jack McCall, including a fictional dime-novel character named Alkali Ike. The event's success inspired the organizers to make it an annual celebration. Over the next few years, they added a theatrical production, brought in Oglala Lakotas from Pine Ridge Indian Reservation, and expanded the rodeo. National publicity came when President Coolidge attended and donned an Indian headdress in 1927. Over the years the Days of '76 has focused more on the rodeo and extended its run to several days.

Trial of Jack McCall: After the first celebration ended, the promoters realized they could use historical re-enactors and the Trial of Jack McCall as ongoing summer attractions. They turned three local people into surrogates for past icons. Poker Alice Tubbs, the cigar-smoking gambler and brothel madam from Sturgis, became the stand-in for Calamity Jane. Deadwood Dick Clark, named after a dime-novel character, portrayed a frontier scout reminiscent of Wild Bill. When Tubbs and Clark died in 1930, the city turned to Potato Creek Johnny as the next representative of Deadwood's frontier past. Johnny had found a large gold nugget and appeared to be a true-to-life prospector. When he died in 1943, he was buried with honors next to Wild Bill at Mount Moriah Cemetery. While many of Deadwood's famous personalities made it to Mount Moriah, Poker Alice was buried in Sturgis and Deadwood Dick was laid to rest on top of Sunrise Mountain, just behind the Lodge at Deadwood.

Rodeo Grounds: The rodeo grounds were built in an area that once housed several gold mills. Some of them, such as the Golden Reward's cyanide plant, operated until escalating costs during World War I forced its closure. The mills that sat next to the rodeo grounds were, however, less successful, and they closed some years before the Golden Reward, leaving behind mill tailings and dilapidated buildings. When Deadwood's mayor and city park committee decided to build an amusement park in 1914, they chose the recently abandoned location. Despite the industrial waste, it had the space they needed for a racetrack, sports fields, an ice-skating rink, a swimming pool, and a grandstand. They tore down buildings and leveled the ground, accomplishing the last task using the sand they found in the nearby waste piles and in the waste the Homestake dumped in the creek. As the amusement park then went up, some Deadwood residents groused about how far it was from the main part of town. It succeeded nonetheless, especially as it began to draw tourists in the 1920s. Wishing to attract even more visitors, city boosters added amenities such as a dancing pavilion in 1923.

When the Deadwood Business Club sponsored the first Days of '76 in 1924, it used the amusement park. As the Days of '76 grew, the old grandstands proved inadequate. By the time Depression-era work relief became available, the city was ready to replace them. The federal government agreed to support the project, and WPA workers, under the supervision of the Juso Brothers, replaced the antiquated grandstands with the current log-framed structure in 1937. The Juso Brothers had brought traditional Finnish log building techniques to the Black Hills. The *Deadwood Pioneer-Times* described the brothers as the "outstanding log workers in the Black Hills Country." They built over fifty log structures in the northern Black Hills. The cabin behind the Days of '76 Museum is another example of their work. Deadwood preservation money keeps the log grandstands structurally sound.

Days of '76 Museum: As the parade grew, the organizers acquired more and more vintage vehicles, clothing, memorabilia, and archival material. They stored the collection in a pole barn, which also served as a small museum. In 1990, the city acquired Don Clowser's collection of western materials that he had collected while operating the "Trading Post" on Deadwood's Main Street. Those artifacts were also placed in the Days of '76 Museum. The pole barn could not adequately house the growing collection, and the Days of '76 committee began advocating for a new building. In 2004, they received a boost when the city provided a major grant. It still took time to gather enough money to build the museum, but in 2013, Deadwood History Inc., the organization that took over management, held a grand opening.

Fire scars: A careful examination of the hillsides to the south and east shows evidence of the 1959 and 2002 forest fires that burned close to Deadwood, threatening its existence.

Part Ten Up Deadwood Gulch

Route Overview: Leave lower Deadwood, turn left (west). Travel through Deadwood on Pioneer Way, US 14A, toward Central City. Turn south onto Aqueduct Avenue and stop between the Homestake/Barrick Gold office and the Lawrence County Highway Department building for a Recommended Stop.

Mileage starts at First Discovery of Gold marker on Crescent Drive in lower Deadwood.

0.0 mi **Lower Deadwood: Turn left onto US 14A and travel toward Central City.**

1.7 mi **Broken Boot Gold Mine:** Olaf Seim and James Nelson staked a claim at this location in 1878. Given its proximity to the Homestake vein, they hoped to make a big gold find, but that did not happen. While they uncovered some gold, it was not enough to make a profit. Instead, Seim and Nelson made money by selling iron pyrite, a combination of iron and sulfur, often called fool's gold. The Deadwood

Charles C. McBride's photo of the Deadwood & Delaware Smelting Works in Deadwood, 1890. *South Dakota State Historical Society*

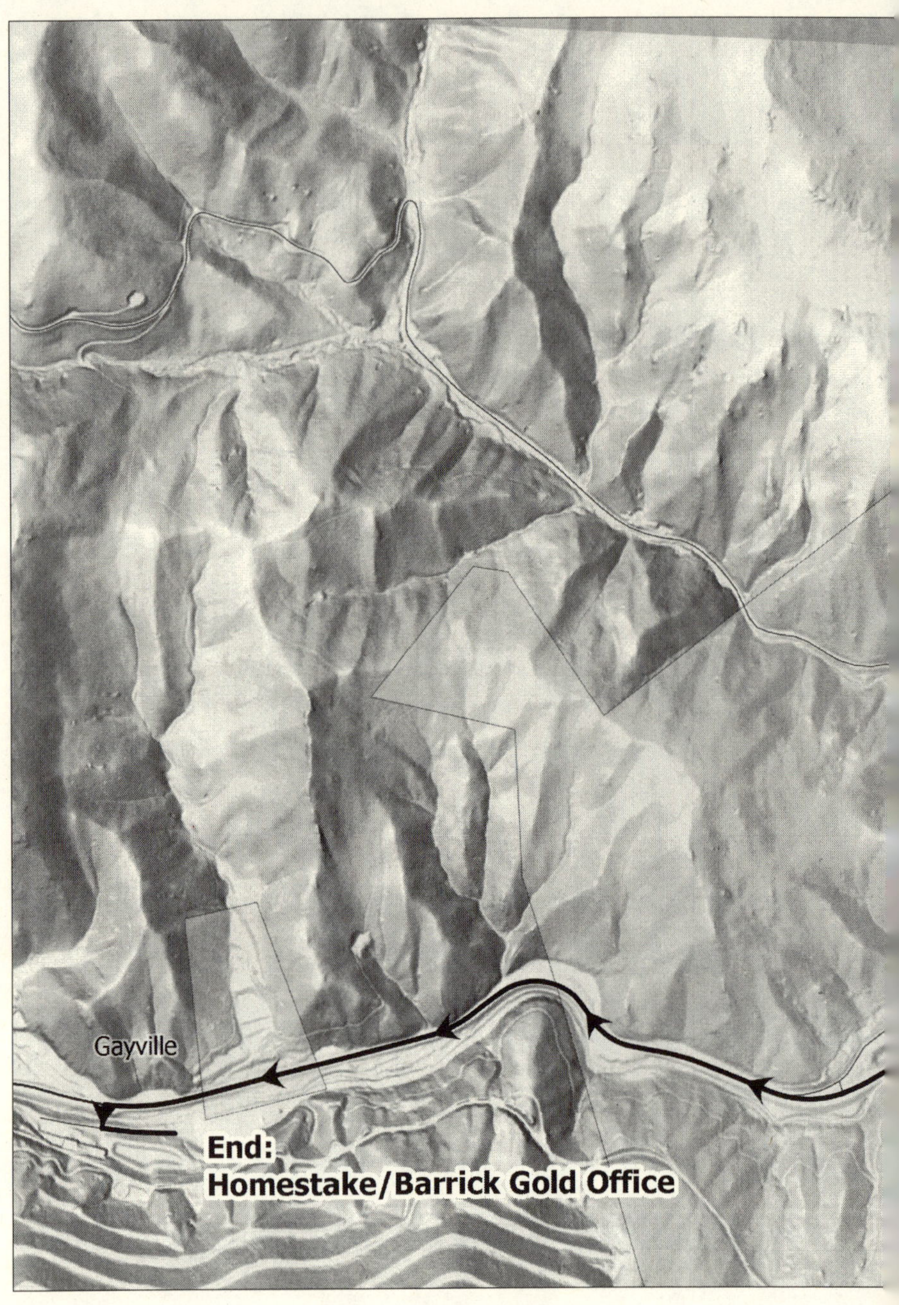
Gayville
End:
Homestake/Barrick Gold Office

BLACK HILLS
NATIONAL
FOREST
Start:
Days of '76 Event Complex
and Rodeo Grounds
Deadwood
14A
85
Esri, NASA, NGA, USGS, FEMA, South Dakota Department of Transportation

and Delaware Smelter used the pyrite as a flux in the smelting process. Known as the Olaf Seim pyrite mine, it shipped about 30,000 tons of pyrite from 1900 to 1901. When the smelter closed in 1902, the mine lost its biggest customer and closed. It reopened briefly during World War I when sulfur was in demand. In 1954, a group of Deadwood businessmen leased the mine to create a tourist attraction. While cleaning and stabilizing it, they found an old boot. The mine became known as the "Broken Boot."

2.5 mi **Recommended Stop on Aqueduct Avenue, between the Barrick Gold office and the Lawrence County Highway Department building on the left.**

Second gold discovery: At this location Blacktail Gulch joins Deadwood Gulch from the north, and what was once Bobtail Gulch joined Deadwood Gulch from the south. Near here a group of prospectors known as the Lardner Party, composed of William Lardner, William and Alfred Gay, and others, found "paying quantities" of gold in early November 1875. Since prospectors had looked for gold near Spruce Gulch in the summer of 1875, this location is often called the second discovery of gold. But the men at Spruce Gulch failed to identify paying quantities of gold, which could make this the first discovery of gold. In either case, the finds in this area proved the richness of the region and started the rush to the northern Black Hills.

Setting the rules: The Lardner Party established the placer mining rules that would apply throughout the region. These regulations were based on traditions developed during prior gold rushes, and then codified into a series of federal laws, including the Mining Law of 1872. The first step was to set up a mining district. The Lardner Party organized the Lost Mining District, the first of four districts that would be created along Whitewood and Deadwood Creeks. They also set the claim size at 300 feet along the creek, and then up the canyon walls from rim to rim, which has sometimes been interpreted as meaning to the top of the mountains. In fact, it meant to the highest level that placer gold might exist. While each prospector was allowed one claim per district, the discoverer got an extra claim. To differentiate the claims, they were numbered, starting from the discovery location and then counting each way, above and below discovery. To make sense of who held what, each district selected a recorder. William Lardner was named recorder for the Lost Mining District. The large claim size, combined with the fact that gold existed in only about six miles of the creeks, allowed around 100 men to claim the entire Whitewood and Deadwood Creek drainages by the second week of January 1876.

Origin of gold: In placer mining, gold is found in alluvial basins, or where sediment is deposited by water. This gold had previously eroded from a gold vein and traveled with the water until it hit an obstruction or came to slower moving water, such as a sandbar or a bend in the creek. The weight of the metal caused it to work its way through the loose gravel to settle on bedrock, which could be several feet deep. Gold pans and picks are often associated with prospectors, but these were used primarily for sampling and clean-up. Once a prospector had staked a claim, he generally hired a crew to dig to bedrock and then process the gold-bearing gravel in sluice boxes. These six-foot-long, open-top boxes contained wooden cleats to catch the gold and were often connected in a series. Since the wealth in Deadwood Gulch had come from the Homestake vein, the richest claims were found just below where it outcropped, near the junction of Deadwood and Blacktail Gulches. Claim Number 2, just below this location, shipped as much as $150,000 of gold in six months.

Gayville: Near the site of discovery, members of the Lardner Party set up Gayville, named after party member William Gay. While it was not officially platted or organized, it can be seen as the region's first town. Like all early mining camps, Gayville had some exciting times. One of its most dramatic moments came when two men broke into Jack Hinch's room and killed him in his sleep on 9 July 1876. Hinch had previously warned an unsuspecting card player that the men had been cheating him, and they wanted revenge. One of the killers was quickly apprehended and put on trial before a miners' court, where prospectors served as a jury. Because of the heinous crime and the notoriety of the people involved, such a large crowd gathered that the trial had to be held in the street. The spectators were divided between

The cyanide sand treatment plant in Gayville, 1908.
South Dakota State Historical Society

those who wanted to hang the accused and those who wished to set him free. Violence was only averted when the district recorder threatened to shoot anyone who caused trouble. In the end, the jury found the suspect guilty of assault and battery. Since there were no jails, and a person could not be hanged for assault and battery, the judge banished him. The next day, 2 August, a large group of men escorted him out of town. Instead of making sure he left, the escorts were his friends, ensuring that vigilantes didn't string him up. Hinch's killing has been called the first homicide of the diggings. Despite such notoriety and an advantageous location, Gayville failed to grow. When the camp burned in May 1886, it never recovered.

Bobtail Gulch: At one time, Bobtail Gulch came into Deadwood Gulch near this location from the south. Today it is filled with overburden from the Homestake's open pit operations of the 1980s.

In the early days of the gold rush, Bobtail Gulch attracted many prospectors, including Fred and Moses Manuel and their partners.

They searched for hardrock or quartz outcroppings, correctly guessing that the region's placer gold originated nearby. The Manuels had already located the Golden Terry Mine, but they continued to look for more promising claims. In early April 1876, as the snow began to melt, Moses searched the ridge above Bobtail Gulch. On 8 April, he found a promising quartz outcropping on the north fork of Gold Run Creek. He took some samples to camp and crushed and panned them. The results looked good. The next day, Moses and one of his partners, Hank Harney, staked the Homestake claim. They chose that name because they thought it would yield enough money to get them home. Word quickly spread, and more prospectors staked claims from Lead to Central City along what became known as the Homestake vein or belt. As the Manuels worked their claim, George Hearst, a successful mining man with holdings in California, Nevada, and Utah, heard about the discoveries. With his curiosity piqued, he sent L. D. Kellogg, an experienced miner, to verify the wealth. Kellogg was impressed, and he bonded the Homestake claim. Hearst then came to the Black Hills and closed the sale in October 1877, paying about $70,000 for the Homestake and an adjacent claim. He incorporated the mine one month later. From then on, Hearst and his partners, J. B. Haggin and Lloyd Tevis, began acquiring every claim and mine along the vein, but it took time as some companies resisted. Their most formidable competitor was the Father DeSmet Mine, which controlled the north end of the outcropping, across from Central City. It took a while, but Hearst finally captured that mine as well as every other property by the early 1880s.

Terraville: As the extent of the Homestake outcropping became evident, a town known as Terraville was started at the head of Bobtail Gulch, about midway along the vein. It took its name from the neighboring Terra Mine. Houses, stores, saloons, and churches hung from the hillsides, while two large gold mills sat at the bottom of Bobtail Gulch. With a strong industrial base, Terraville grew to about 700 people by 1890, making it the third-largest gold camp at that time, trailing only Lead and Deadwood. When the price of gold went up, the Homestake decided to mine the edges of the open cut, recovering low-grade ore that it had previously ignored. The company bought out the Terraville homeowners and closed the town in 1982. It then dumped waste rock into Bobtail Gulch, covering the townsite.

Blacktail Gulch: Just below Central City, to the north of Deadwood Gulch, is Blacktail Gulch. Maitland Road and Blacktail Road are located within the gulch. Some placer gold was found along Blacktail Creek, and gold ore was uncovered on the hillsides. This area's ore was classified as conglomerate, meaning geologic pressure had caused placer gold to recombine with country rock. Several small mines and mills opened, producing a fair amount of gold. The Columbus Consolidated is perhaps the most famous. Its mill sat at the mouth of Blacktail Gulch and appears in many historic photographs. Gold deposits in the gulch did not extend very deep and played out quickly. Most of the conglomerate mines closed by the early 1880s. Some unscrupulous mine owners tried to sell their properties to the unsuspecting. The most famous case of fraud came when the Esmeralda operatives featured their large mill on stock certificates in order to sell more shares, but they said nothing about nonexistent ore reserves.

Mine disputes: Competition among so many companies for a limited amount of gold ore resulted in numerous disputes. The most famous incident happened in Hidden Treasure Gulch, just north of Central City, in September 1877. It started when miners in the Keets and Aurora Mines crossed into each other's underground workings. A fight started, soon spreading to the surface and escalating into a gun battle. When Cephas Tuttle, one of the Aurora's owners, was killed, Sheriff Bullock interceded. He blamed the Keets miners and arrested nearly every one of them.

In a separate incident, also involving the Keets property, the miners went on strike to protest unpaid wages in November 1877. After they took control of the mine, Sheriff Bullock again appeared on the scene. Failing to persuade the miners to leave, he convinced the governor to send troops. In the end, they only watched as Bullock lowered a stink bomb down a ventilation shaft, driving the men out of the mine.

Homestake Sand Plant: When the cyanide process for treating gold ore was developed, the Homestake built a cyanide plant, or what was called a sand plant, in Gayville/Central City in 1902. It operated until 1934. After closing the plant, the Homestake turned it over to the Lead American Legion, and the members placed an ice rink measuring 60 feet by 360 feet inside. The rink lasted until the building was demolished in 1965. The concrete foundations remain, with the office of Homestake/Barrick Gold sitting on part of them.

Towns in Deadwood Gulch: Besides Gayville, a series of towns developed along Deadwood Creek. South Bend, Central City, and Golden Gate all came into existence above Gayville in 1876–1877. A Deadwood paper stated that although the three camps were virtually next to each other, the residents insisted on maintaining their towns' identities. Even so, the camps were generally viewed as part of Central City by the mid-1880s.

South Bend: The gold camp of South Bend sat near the mouth of Blacktail Gulch and could count 500 people and thirteen businesses, including three saloons, by 1878. As the mines in Blacktail Gulch played out, South Bend lost its importance, and the census taker found only 116 residents there in 1880. Central City absorbed it soon after.

Central City: Just as its name implies, this camp sat at the center of the action. The Homestake vein outcropped to its south; conglomerate mines opened to the north. Several stamp mills went up nearby. Most importantly, the Father DeSmet Mine, working the northern end of the Homestake vein, built its sixty-stamp mill across from the town. Cabins first appeared in Central City by November 1875, and many more followed as the population grew to about 3,000 by 1880, making it the second-largest gold camp at that time. A wide variety of businesses naturally followed. A fire destroyed much of Central City in April 1888, however, and the town never fully recovered. Lead had become the dominant gold camp, and some of the former residents moved there. Only about 500 people remained by 1890.

Central City in 1876. *South Dakota State Historical Society*

Golden Gate: Golden Gate sat just above Central City. Though it had the same advantages as Central City, located on the north end of the Homestake vein and next to the conglomerate mines, it never developed to the same degree and soon became part of its larger neighbor.

Anchor City: Next to Golden Gate, at the mouth of Poorman Gulch, a small location known as Anchor City popped up. Several mines opened nearby, but these were slightly removed from the best mining ground and failed to prosper. Anchor City did attract a small population and a few businesses, but it became indistinguishable from Golden Gate and Central City early on.

Railroad in Deadwood Gulch: The Fremont, Elkhorn & Missouri Valley Railroad built from Deadwood through Central City and on to the Bald Mountain and Ruby Basin Mining Districts in 1891. This line hauled ore from the mines to the processing plants in lower Deadwood. The Elkhorn also built a line from Central City to Lead in 1901. To reach Lead, the railroad dug a large cut in the hillside across the gulch from Maitland Road. The cut is still evident just up the gulch from the Homestake/Barrick office.

County poor farm: In 1888, Lawrence County purchased an old placer claim near Gayville and established a county poor farm. The commissioners believed that instead of providing individual relief it was more appropriate to have a place of "refuge for the poor." It operated until about 1956. The KOA campground sits next to a former poor farm building.

Part Eleven The Wharf Gold Mine

Route Overview: From the Second Discovery of Gold location, take US 14A to the west. After 0.3 miles, leave US 14A and follow Central City's Main Street through downtown. Return to US 14A after 0.6 miles and follow it through upper Lead. Once at Nevada Gulch Road, turn right (north). Follow Nevada Gulch Road to the top of the mountain for a Recommended Stop at the visitor platform of the Wharf Mine.

Mileage starts at Second Discovery of Gold location.

0.0 mi **Second Discovery of Gold location: Return to US 14A and travel west.**

0.1 mi **Maitland Road:** Maitland Road connects US 14A with the northern edge of the Black Hills. Maitland Road is not part of the tour, but there are sites along it that are relevant to the gold rush. A few of those are mentioned below.

Maitland Road parallels Blacktail Creek for about a mile. Prospectors found placer gold in Blacktail Creek, but the creek is small and the amount of gold was limited. This gold had eroded from the Homestake vein, and sometimes had recombined with the country rock, creating what was called conglomerate ore or paleo-placers. The hillsides along Blacktail Creek contained a good amount of this ore. Multiple mining companies dug shafts to reach the ore and built stamp mills to crush and treat it. Companies such as the Imperial and the Esmeralda had success operating in the gulch during the first decades of Black Hills mining, but with so little gold the mines played out fairly quickly. Still wanting to profit, the mine owners sometimes sold stock based on false promises and skipped town with the proceeds. One of the more famous scams involved the Esmeralda Mine. Its mill sat on a piece of flat ground that is still evident half a mile up the gulch, on the left. Rock waste piles from other mining operations can also be seen along Maitland Road until it turns sharply to the right and begins the climb out of the gulch.

Maitland Road eventually crosses a divide and enters the drainage of False Bottom Creek. There are two explanations as to how this creek gained its name. One story says that prospectors who had searched the creek in vain for placer gold spread a rumor that it had a "false bottom," meaning the gold sat on a rock layer below what had been previously prospected. More digging belied the rumor, but the name stuck. A second, less interesting account is based on the fact that the water in the creek disappears into the limestone creek bed. The creek only carries water its entire length during wet years. While this could be the source of its name, many Black Hills creeks disappear in a similar fashion.

After a little more than three miles, Maitland Road reaches the former townsite of Maitland. Mining operations began there in the late 1800s. Some miners believed they had found an extension of the Homestake vein. Several mines opened, with the largest operation known variously as the Maitland, Penobscot, North Homestake, or Canyon Corporation. A small town formed nearby, and it also went by several names, including Garden City, New Chicago, and Maitland. The last name came from Alexander and S. F. Maitland, Michigan entrepreneurs who invested in the mines in the early twentieth century. At one time a large cyanide mill sat next to the road. The mill's back wall can still be seen along the hillside, all that remains of what was once a good-sized mining and milling operation.

Main tour narrative continues on US 14A.

0.3 mi **Leave US 14A and angle onto Central City's Main Street.**

0.4 mi **St. Lawrence O'Toole Catholic Church, 618 Central Main Street:** Built in Central City's business district in 1879, the St. Lawrence O'Toole Catholic Church survived a devastating fire that destroyed almost 140 structures in 1888. Central City never fully recovered from the fire.

0.5 mi **Hidden Gulch Road, Central City:** A short distance up Hidden Gulch Road, on the right, is the "Central City, Golden Gate and Terraville Hose Co." fire hall. The residents of the three neighboring

BLACK HILLS
NATIONAL
FOREST
End:
Wharf Mine
473

Gayville

Start:
Homestake/
Barrick
Gold Office

Central City

14A

85

Lead

Esri, NASA, NGA, USGS, FEMA, South Dakota Department of Transportation

towns recognized the need for fire protection in the wake of the 1888 disaster and built this fire hall in 1889.

0.7 mi **Turn onto a side street to return to US 14A. Pause at the side street's junction with US 14A to view the two sites listed below.**

Black Hills or Rosenkranz Brewery: The Rosenkranz brewery sat across the creek from Central City. Since it relied on water from Deadwood Creek, the owners located it upstream from where the mining operations fouled the water. After opening in 1877, its Gold Nugget Beer became the region's most popular, especially when the Deadwood fire of 1879 wiped out much of its competition. The brewery, however, struggled as South Dakota wrestled with prohibiting alcohol. The company produced "near beer" between 1889, when South Dakota achieved statehood and implemented prohibition, and 1896, when the law was repealed. The return of prohibition in the 1920s closed the plant for good. To comply with the law, the company dumped all its remaining beer into Deadwood Creek, which reportedly carried a foam head for miles. All that remains of the building is a stone wall partially hidden by bushes.

The Black Hills Brewing Company, ca. 1900–1910. The Father DeSmet Mill is visible on the right; the open cut can be seen in the background. *Black Hills Mining Museum*

Homestake Open Cut/Father DeSmet Mine: The north end of the Homestake open cut is evident to the right (southwest), high on the hill. Prospectors discovered gold all along the Homestake vein in 1876. The Father DeSmet Mining Co. acquired the vein's northern end and built a large stamp mill there. It sat on the level piece of ground that still exists just above US 14A and below the open cut. It competed with the Homestake for mining ground and water, until Homestake operatives acquired it in the early 1880s.

1.3 mi **Deadwood Gulch/Cutting Mine Road:** At this location, US 14A leaves Deadwood Gulch and follows Poorman Gulch to Lead. Cutting Mine Road, on the right, follows Deadwood Gulch. As the road's name implies, it goes past the Cutting or Gladiator Mine. Miners worked this property intermittently from 1900 to 1925, finding more water than gold. The City of Deadwood eventually acquired the property to use as a backup water supply.

1.3 mi **Poorman Gulch:** Two possible explanations exist for the name. According to *South Dakota Geographic Names,* prospector Otto Grantz found the area's gold ore easy to process, without the need of expensive equipment. In other words, a "poorman" could afford to work it. The other possibility comes from Poorman Gulch's lack of placer gold. With an abundance of gold found just below it in Deadwood Gulch, this lack of gold ensured a prospector would stay a "poorman."

1.7 mi **Homestake Jubilee Cabins:** To celebrate the fiftieth anniversary of the mine's discovery, the Homestake recreated an Old West town at this location. The company also built a 9,000-person grandstand where it hosted parades, concerts, and a pageant. Some of the buildings among the Ponderosa Pines tourist cabins were built for the 1926 Jubilee Celebration.

2.1 mi **Lead Roundhouse:** The brick building to the east of US 14A was built as a five-stall roundhouse for the Black Hills & Ft. Pierre Railroad (BH&FtP) in 1901. The Homestake built the narrow gauge railroad to haul mine timbers and cordwood from the forest to the mine,

Revelers enjoy the Homestake Gold Mine Jubilee in Lead, 1926.
South Dakota State Historical Society

beginning in 1881. The BH&FtP had several tracks in Lead, with the area around the roundhouse serving as a service yard. The mining company started constructing the roundhouse in 1899. The Burlington finished it after purchasing the rail line the next year.

2.2 mi **Optional Tour of Lead:** The Gold Rush Tour follows US 14A through the upper portions of Lead. Only a few of the town's locations are discussed. A tour of Lead is included in the Northern Black Hills–Homestake tour.

2.2 mi **Homestake Mine Manager's House:** To the right (west) of US 14A is the Homestake Mine manager's house. Large mining companies often provided homes for their managers, and the Homestake was no different. It not only served as a luxury residence, but also as a place to entertain. Built in 1933, this home replaced an earlier one that was next to the mine. The last manager to live here moved out in 1979. The company then used it for meetings and sold it not long after.

2.3 mi **Junction with US 85: Continue on US 14A/US 85 to the west.**

3.4 mi **US 14A/US 85 intersects Nevada Gulch Road: Turn right (north) onto Nevada Gulch Road, Lawrence County Road 473.**

3.7 mi **Nevada Gulch School:** The headquarters for the Mickelson Trail is in the building on the left, to the west. It served as a school into the 1960s.

3.9 mi **Inferno Bar location**: A 3.2 beer joint (a bar that serves beer with only 3.2 percent alcohol, a legacy of prohibition) known as the Inferno existed inside a large mine cavern at this location. Operating from 1950 until about 1978, its unique atmosphere made it a popular place, especially during special events, such as the Days of '76. At times the bar sponsored concerts in the parking lot, forcing cars to park up and down the gulch. Since closing, people have talked about reopening it, but because of health and safety concerns it will probably remain closed.

5.1 mi **Nevada Gulch Road:** This road travels through the Black Hills' second-most important gold region, which comprises the Bald Mountain and Ruby Basin Mining Districts. Several mines operated in the area west of the road from the early 1890s into the 1910s. A couple of rail lines also built through, with one running up Nevada Gulch. Evidence of the historic mining and railroad operations has mostly disappeared. As the road ascends the hill, the Golden Reward's reclaimed mine site from the 1980s can be seen. A few years ago, the Wharf Mine reworked some of this area. To do this, it re-routed Nevada Gulch Road and installed large culverts to allow haul trucks to travel under the road. The Wharf's haul road is now blocked, but the culverts remain.

6.6 mi **Turn right toward the Wharf Mine on Stewart Slope Road.**

6.7 mi **Town of Trojan:** Ground depressions and old foundations can be seen along both sides of the road. These are reminders of the town of Trojan. Its history is covered at the Wharf platform stop.

6.8 mi **Recommended Stop at Wharf platform, Coeur-Wharf Mine.**

Platform signage: While the Wharf Gold Mine's current operations have moved beyond what is easily visible from the platform, the company has installed signage that explains the gold mining process.

Background and technique: A Canadian mining company started the Wharf Mine as the price of gold rose in the 1980s. It eventually sold to Goldcorp, a large Canadian company. Goldcorp sold to Coeur in 2015, a relatively small mining company headquartered in Chicago. In 2020, it operated three mines in the United States and one in Mexico, but it plans to expand.

The Wharf Mine began operations on the western edge of the historic Bald Mountain Mining District, near the headwaters of Annie Creek. Prospectors originally discovered ore there and created the Reliance Mining Company in 1897. Finding the ore difficult to treat, the owners built a cyanide plant in 1906, which produced 27,000 ounces of gold before closing in 1915. The property was explored over the years that followed, including during the Depression, but was not reopened until the price of gold went up and modern mining practices became available in the 1980s. From its original Annie Creek pit, the Wharf Mine steadily advanced eastward, reworking properties that had been mined in the late nineteenth and early twentieth centuries. As the operators opened and reclaimed each pit, they gave it a name reminiscent of a historic mine, such as Portland, Foley, and Trojan. The company recently finished mining the Green Mountain pit and reclaiming the American Eagle pit. It has moved into locations known as the Portland Ridge and Boston Expansion.

Coeur-Wharf operates the last large-scale gold mine in the Black Hills, using techniques that have become standard across the industry: drilling test holes, evaluating gold content, plotting the course of development, blasting, separating overburden from ore, hauling waste away and ore to a crusher, dumping ore on leach pads, treating the ore with cyanide, removing the gold from the solution, and sending the end product to a refinery. When all the gold has been recovered, the leach pads are off-loaded and the open pits are filled in with the processed ore.

Production: In 2023, the Wharf Mine produced 93,502 ounces of gold and 267,786 ounces of silver. With gold averaging about $1,940.50 per ounce in 2023, the gold produced would value over $181,440,000. Silver was near $23 per ounce, which would yield about $6,159,000. The total revenue should guarantee a handsome profit, but gold and silver prices are quite volatile. The mine operated when gold sold from $240 to $600 per ounce, which made it difficult to stay open. The company currently employs about 250 people. Since 1982, the Wharf has probably produced around three to four million ounces of gold. The Homestake, for comparison, produced about 41 million ounces in its 124 years of operation. When the Wharf started, the life of the mine was projected to be seven years, but like many modern mines, it has added years as it has expanded. In a quest for more ore, and considering today's high gold prices, the company continues to advance into new ground and to reopen areas that it had previously reclaimed. Mining is currently projected to continue until 2028.

Early Mining/Trojan/Portland: Historically, this area has been part of the Bald Mountain Mining District. When miners discovered gold here in 1877, assay values detected good gold content, but the gold could not be recovered. Unlike the Homestake's free-milling ore, this ore is refractory, meaning that the gold is chemically bound to the rock. The history of the area therefore revolved around finding a process to effectively treat the ore.

Despite the problems, investors consolidated a few claims, built a mill, and formed the Portland Mining Company in 1880. A small camp called Portland followed, growing to a population of 229, but not until a smelter and chlorination plant opened in Deadwood and the Elkhorn Railroad built into this area could the gold be recovered at a profit. The Portland company began shipping ore to Deadwood in the 1890s. The introduction of the cyanide process brought even more development. The American Eagle Company replaced the Portland Co. in 1906 and built a cyanide mill near the mine. It was then absorbed by the Trojan Company in 1911. The Trojan Co. acquired more property and expanded the mill, operating successfully until high costs and low gold prices forced it to close in 1923. Around these

The Bald Mountain Mill in 1970, before it was destroyed by the Wharf Mine's expansion. *Author photo*

companies the town of Trojan formed, becoming indistinguishable from Portland.

Investors purchased the Trojan's property and formed the Bald Mountain Mining Company in 1928. Despite exploring the property, they did not open the mine until 1934 when the price of gold increased from $20 to $35 per ounce. Bald Mountain continued to operate until the government deemed gold mines a non-essential industry during World War II and ordered them closed. Unlike most area mines, the Bald Mountain Mine reopened after the war and ran intermittently from 1945 to 1959. Once mining ended, a tourist attraction called Top of the Hills operated for one year.

The Town of Trojan: Through most of its existence, Trojan had a few hundred people, a handful of stores, a few saloons, and a school. But as people left, the school closed and the town became derelict. Some people hung on until the Wharf bought their property in the 1980s and 1990s. The one feature that persisted was a red two-story schoolhouse. It served as a ski lodge for a time, and when modern mining began, it provided office space for mining companies, including the Wharf. As the Wharf expanded, it removed all reminders of historic mining, such as the Reliance stamp mill, the Dakota Hoist, the Portland Mine, the Bald Mountain Mill, and the town of Trojan. The Trojan school survived, standing by itself on an island of land, until the company demolished it in 2010. While this area never had a large population, it had survived for decades, and many people still trace family connections to Trojan.

The Trojan Schoolhouse, just prior to its demolition in 2010.
Author photo

Part Twelve Terry and the Ruby Basin Mining District

Route Overview: From the Wharf platform, continue west on Wharf Road. Do a loop through the Wharf parking lot/production area then turn around for a return trip on Wharf Road. Return to Nevada Gulch Road. Travel down Nevada Gulch Road to Terry Gulch Road (Fantail Gulch Road). Go up Terry Gulch Road to the Terry townsite for a Recommended Stop.

Mileage starts at Wharf platform.

0.0 mi **Wharf platform: Travel west on Wharf Road.**

0.8 mi **Gate for haul road: The tour crosses the mine's haul road and enters an active mine site. The gate is activated with an electric sensor**.

0.9 mi **Richmond Hill Road intersection**:
Follow the Wharf Road as it veers to the left.

1.6 mi **Richmond Hill Mine:** A reclaimed waste pile is visible in the distance north of the road. It is from the Richmond Hill open pit gold mine that operated in the 1980s. Barrick Gold currently controls the site and oversees its reclamation. The mine was developed next to the historic mining district and camp of Carbonate.

Carbonate: Three miles north of Wharf Road is the Carbonate silver district. In 1881, James Redpath (sometimes spelled Ridpath) discovered carbonate silver ore, started the West Virginia Mine, and organized the Carbonate Mining District. A small camp called West Virginia (later shortened to Virginia), after Redpath's home state, soon followed. Problems in treating the ore hampered operations. Better times came when the Iron Hill Company developed a mine and opened a smelter in 1885. When silver bars began appearing in

Mine ruins at Carbonate, 2018. *Author photo*

Deadwood, many companies sprang into action, and the town of Carbonate came into existence. Several thousand people reportedly lived there, supporting a wide variety of businesses. The boom began turning into a bust in 1887 as the silver played out. The Iron Hill Mine, under the direction of Seth Bullock, tried to find more silver but failed, as did the rest of the mines. Most closed by the early 1890s. Today, open mine shafts and piles of waste rock can still be found, but the town's location has become an open meadow. Other reminders of the camp include a cemetery and pieces of a small smelter in Rubicon Gulch, a little below the mines. One story associated with the camp claims that arsenic-ladened smelter smoke killed all the cats. The smelter sat some distance from town, making the incident unlikely. The development of the Richmond Hill Mine blocked easy access to the Carbonate area.

2.4 mi **Wharf parking lot, with a view of the gold leaching piles:** The Wharf office, service yard, and ore processing area can be seen from the parking lot. The large piles of rock are part of the heap leach-

Start:
Wharf Mine
473

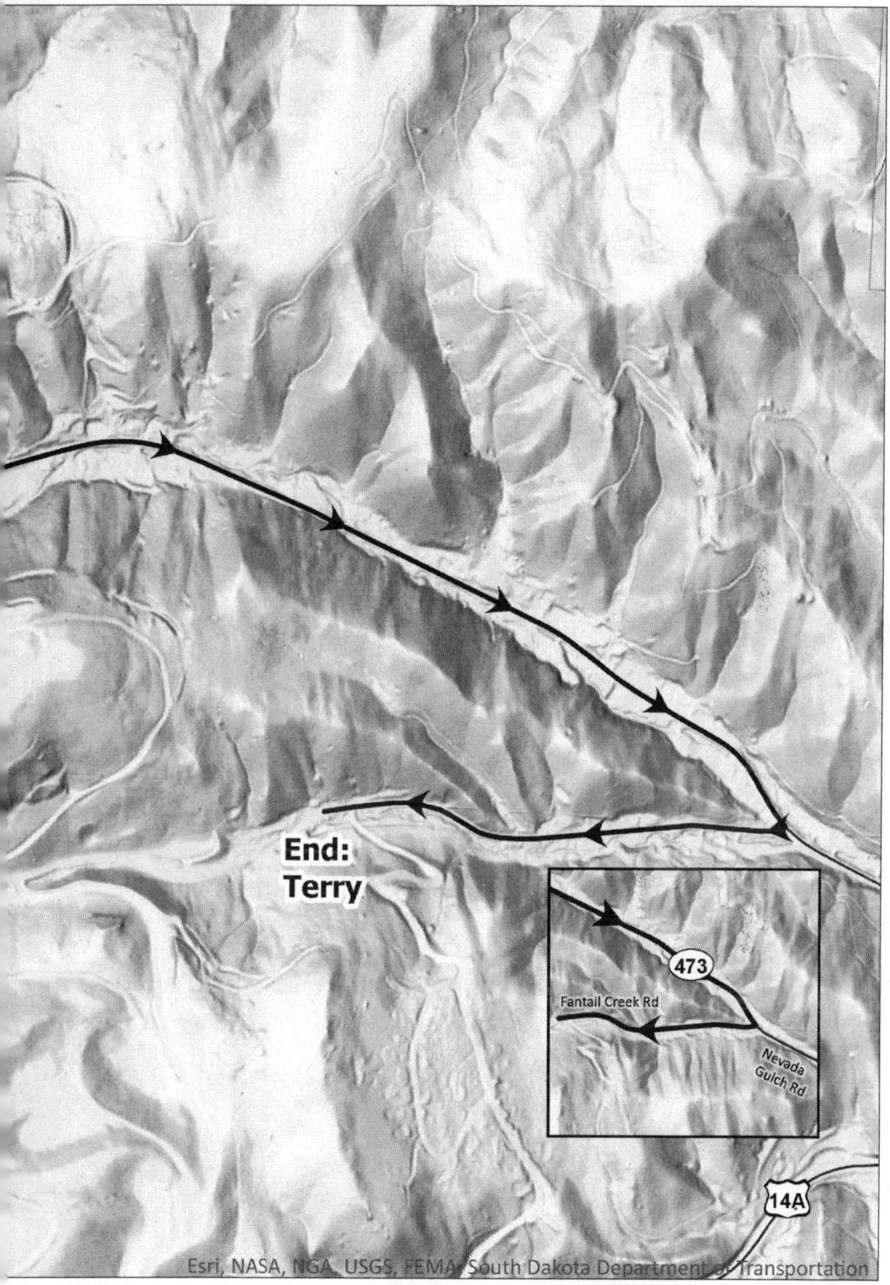

End:
Terry

473

Fantail Creek Rd

Nevada Gulch Rd

14A

Esri, NASA, NGA, USGS, FEMA, South Dakota Department of Transportation

ing operation. The process involves piling ore on thick plastic liners, draping plastic tubes over the top, and dripping cyanide through it to dissolve the gold. As the cyanide/gold solution runs off, it is captured, and the gold is recovered. The cyanide is then reused. Once the process is completed, the spent ore is removed and returned to open pits as part of the reclamation process.

Preston, Balmoral, Cyanide, and Ragged Top: A trail heads north out of the Wharf parking lot to the Ragged Top Mining District and the towns of Preston, Balmoral, Cyanide, and Ragged Top. Prospectors found gold around Ragged Top Mountain in 1896. A fairly large mill was built at Cyanide in 1902, but the boom turned to bust by 1906. During its brief boom, the region's population grew to nearly 400 people, and the towns gained several buildings, a few of which remained until recently, including a school. The skeleton of a two-story still stood in 2021, and a cemetery is hidden in the woods.

The gold around Ragged Top Mountain apparently was in pockets and close to the surface, accounting for the mines' brief productive period. A company recently requested permission to mine the area for remaining gold. Since the operations would be near Spearfish Canyon, the promoters proposed a small operation. Public outcry, however, persuaded the Lawrence County commissioners to deny the necessary permits.

Ragged Top Mountain in 2018. The towns of Preston, Cyanide, and Ragged Top sat around it. *Author photo*

After the loop through the Wharf lot, head east on Wharf Mine Road.

2.6–2.8 mi **Railroad bed evidence:** The Wharf Mine has destroyed nearly all signs of historic mining and railroading, but some faint reminders still exist. For instance, the Wharf service road parallels roadbeds from the Elkhorn and Burlington Railroad branch lines. The roadbeds are on the north side of the road and appear as slightly elevated pieces of flat ground.

3.8 mi **Gate on the Wharf Mine Road.**

4.9 mi **Junction of Wharf Mine Road and Nevada Gulch Road: Continue south, downhill on Nevada Gulch Road.**

5.2 mi **Terry Peak Ski Area:** Terry Peak Ski Area lies to the west of the road. It began in 1938 when the Bald Mountain Ski Club put in a rope tow, although cross-country skiing had been going on for some time. Several members of the ski club served in World War II, including Ed Keene, who was part of the famed 10th Mountain Division. After the war, members of the division founded dozens of new ski resorts around the United States and developed improved equipment, thereby popularizing the U.S. ski industry. Keene and other veterans organized the Terry Peak Ski Area, with the goal of putting in a chair lift—another 10th Mountain innovation—which they finally accomplished in 1954. Today the ski area contains 600 acres and twenty-five trails. For a time it had a ski jump, but a short, flat landing area made it dangerous and it was eventually removed. The Black Hills' uncertain snowfall has also caused problems, forcing the operators to rely on artificial snow.

Since the ski area exists in a mining area, mining companies have been involved in its development. The Wharf owns part of the enterprise and has spent at least $15 million on facility upgrades, including a new lodge and road improvements. The ski area also uses ponds the Golden Reward Mine built for gold recovery to store water for snow making.

Ed Keene skiing at Terry Peak. *South Dakota State Historical Society*

6.0 mi **Evidence of Golden Reward Mine operations:** The road goes from the Bald Mountain Mining District into the Ruby Basin Mining District. A number of mines operated in the Ruby Basin area during the late nineteenth and early twentieth centuries. Most evidence of past mining activity disappeared when the Golden Reward developed its open pit mine in the 1980s. Part of that open pit operation is visible to the west.

7.8 mi **Junction of Nevada Gulch Road and Terry Gulch (Fantail Gulch) Road: Turn right (north) on Terry Gulch Road.** An early name for this gulch was "Fantail," referring to a type of deer that supposedly lived in the area.

8.3 mi **Gate on Terry Gulch Road, Wharf Mine:**
At this point, the road enters the Wharf Mine's property. The gate is generally open during the summer. If it is open, drive another 0.3 miles for a Recommended Stop at Terry. If it is closed, this location will work for the Recommended Stop.

8.6 mi **Recommended Stop at Terry:** A good place to stop is just before the road's sharp right turn. This is the approximate location of the lower end of the former mining town of Terry.

Ruby Basin Mining District: Terry Gulch Road goes into what was once the heart of the Ruby Basin Mining District. The district sat to the east of Terry Peak, and extended about two miles east and west, and one mile north and south. While gold discoveries were made in 1876–1877, with estimates running up to a half ounce of gold per ton, the ore was refractory and could not be treated with the available recovery processes. Nevertheless, over 400 claims were staked, but little development happened. The area finally thrived when smelting, chlorination, and cyanidation came along beginning in 1888, although most of the treatment plants sat in Deadwood. Mining lasted until 1918, when World War I inflation made costs for labor and supplies too high, especially with the price of gold fixed at $20.67 per ounce. Several mining companies did well, but they still produced far less gold than the Homestake.

The Golden Reward and the Deadwood & Delaware: Four companies came to control most of the mines in the Ruby Basin Mining District: the Golden Reward, the Deadwood & Delaware (D&D), the Horseshoe-Mogul, and the Lundberg, Dorr & Wilson, but over time the Golden Reward came to dominate. In 1887, Harris Franklin bought several claims on the ridge west of Fantail Gulch, including the Golden Reward, Isadorah, Harmony, and Stewart, and organized the Golden Reward Company. Three years later he built a small chlorination plant in Deadwood, followed by a larger plant in 1892. The success of these operations allowed Franklin and his partners to buy more claims, open more mines, and dig several shafts. By 1899, the Golden Reward had 176 employees. One of the company's most productive shafts was the Tornado, located in downtown Terry.

Another important company was the D&D. It bought property in the district to ensure an ore supply for its Deadwood smelter, which ultimately produced $11 million in gold. The D&D sold to the Golden Reward in 1899, nearly doubling that company's holdings. The advent of the cyanide process brought increased gold recovery and a boost to the region in the early twentieth century. The Golden Reward quit relying on chlorination and smelting and built a cyanide plant in Deadwood. By the time it closed in 1918, the Golden Reward had become the second-largest gold producer in the Black Hills, yielding $21 million of gold.

Lundberg, Dorr & Wilson: Three local mining men, John Lundberg, John V. N. Dorr, and A. D. Wilson, also built a cyanide plant in Fantail Gulch, just below the town of Terry, in 1904. Under Dorr's direction the plant became one of the most innovative in the country. Dorr used the knowledge he had gained to build gold mills outside of the Black Hills, earning a national reputation as a leader in the treatment of gold ore.

The Horseshoe-Mogul Company: Located on the western edge of the Ruby Basin Mining District, the Horseshoe Company consolidated several claims and built the Kildonan chlorination plant in Pluma in 1895. The company failed to profit, however, and sold to promoters who had fraud on their minds. To persuade people to invest in what they portrayed as a vast mining operation, the new owners started building a mammoth cyanide plant close to Terry Peak, remodeled the Kildonan mill in Pluma, and bought a smelter in Rapid City. After bilking hundreds of thousands of dollars out of investors, the conmen fled. People who believed in the mining ground took control and finished a downsized version of the cyanide plant in 1903. Just as profit seemed at hand, the plant burned, forcing the company to reorganize. Renamed the Mogul Company, the managers built a new cyanide plant near Terry in 1905 and operated it successfully until 1918.

Modern Mining: After mining came to an end in the 1910s, the Ruby Basin district sat dormant for about seventy years, except for some flurries of exploration. The Anaconda Copper Company of Butte, Montana, acquired the Golden Reward property in the early 1940s. Over the next forty years either Anaconda or the Homestake periodically explored it, though nothing resulted. Then Moruya Gold of Australia paid Anaconda $6 million for 5,000 acres and explored the area in 1985–1986. This company found success, primarily because of higher gold prices, and started mining in 1988, using the historic Golden Reward name. After producing 280,000 ounces of gold and 365,000 ounces of silver, operations ceased in 1996. The company did limited reclamation, leaving the property in a "ready state" in case rising gold prices made mining profitable again. The Wharf purchased the property in 1999, reclaimed it in 2003, and reopened a small portion of the ground about ten years later. That activity has since ended.

Terry: The town of Terry sat at the center of the Ruby Basin Mining District. Three railroads ran through it: the Deadwood Central came up the gulch; the Elkhorn built along the hillsides; and the Burlington had a station just above the town on the side of Terry Peak. The peak was named after General Alfred Terry, commander of the Department of Dakota in 1874. Terry Peak is the sixth-highest mountain in the Black Hills at 7,071 feet.

Like Lead City, Terry had a very diverse population. Reports state that twenty-three nationalities, including several Chinese, lived there. According to census data, Terry boasted 500 people in 1895 and more than doubled to 1,188 in 1900. It peaked in 1904 at 1,200, declined to 1,100 the following year, and saw a brief uptick, with 1,177 in 1910. After the Golden Reward closed in April 1918, Terry lost half its population, dwindling to 531 in 1920 and 174 in 1925.

Community activities: Terry was never officially organized or platted as a townsite. The county government provided law enforcement, but the mining companies, especially the Golden Reward, had a large say in its affairs. Terry had its problems, including some violence, but it lacked Deadwood's boomtown environment. The fact that it was established well after the gold rush ended helps explain this, but the mining companies also played a part. They wanted law and order. A school district was organized in 1891 and counted over 200 students after a few years. The town also had two newspapers, the *Terry Record* and the *Bald Mountain News*. They merged into the *Terry News-Record* in 1904. Residents organized a volunteer fire department as well as five fraternal orders, including the Masons. The Western Federation of Miners, a regional miners' union, started Lodge No. 5 in Terry in 1891. It grew to what was described as the "most prosperous branch" in the Black Hills, with 650 members —60 percent of Terry's population—in 1899. The members built a two-story union hall, with a reading room and a library. The union, however, came to an end with a 1909–1910 lockout of the workers. The Homestake initiated the lockout, wishing to kill the union at its mine, and the smaller companies followed suit. The mines remained closed until the union men either left or swore that they would never join a union again. As far as businesses, the town had three hotels, three restaurants, four saloons, two lawyers, two doctors, and an assortment of general merchandise stores, including one run by a W. H. Disney.

Calamity Jane: Terry may be best known for Calamity Jane Canary dying there in the Calloway Hotel in early August 1903. She had been living in Terry for a week, and reportedly succumbed to inflammation of the bowels. An organization known as the Black Hills Pioneers took charge of her remains and interred her next to Wild Bill Hickok in Deadwood's Mount Moriah Cemetery.

Terry's Demise: Most of Terry disappeared as the mines closed with the approach of World War I, but a few people continued to live there. Since the mining companies owned the mineral rights and the property, the residents signed leases with the Golden Reward, Anaconda, and then Moruya. The leases stated that they could be evicted with thirty days' notice. Fourteen families received eviction notices in early 1986. A great concern was the status of the Terry cemetery. An early plan called for relocating the graves, but as the mining plan evolved, the cemetery remained undisturbed.

Optional Side Trip, Terry Cemetery: If you are interested in visiting Terry's cemetery, follow the road up the hill on the right. At the top of the hill, the road follows the divide between Nevada and Terry Gulches. The road is rough, with many good-sized rocks, and should only be attempted with a 4WD or high clearance vehicle. After 0.5 miles, the road splits. The left-hand branch stops at an overlook after 0.1 miles. The overlook gives a view of Terry Peak, Custer Peak, and parts of Terry Gulch where the town once sat. The right-hand road continues to the cemetery. The distance to the cemetery from the start of the road is 1.1 miles, not counting the side trip. Return by the same road to the bottom of the gulch and the Recommended Stop location.

Part Thirteen **Rochford**

Route Overview: From Terry travel down Terry (Fantail) Gulch Road and merge onto Nevada Gulch Road. At the junction with US 85/14A, turn right. Travel west. At the top of the hill, the highway meets North Rochford Road. Turn left onto North Rochford Road and follow it to the town of Rochford for a Recommended Stop.

Mileage starts at the recommended stop location in Terry (Fantail) Gulch. (If the Wharf Mine gate is closed, the mileage calculation will be off by 0.5–0.6 miles.)

0.0 mi **Terry: Travel down Terry (Fantail) Gulch Road.**

0.8 mi **Merge with Nevada Gulch Road.**

1.0 mi **Junction of Nevada Gulch Road and US 85/14A. Turn to the right (west).**

2.0 mi **North Fork of Whitetail Creek:** The highway parallels Whitetail Creek and then crosses it at this location. A dirt road also angles off to the west. The dirt road once followed Whitetail Creek's North Fork, providing access to the western portion of the Ruby Basin Mining District, but it is currently blocked. This part of the district was not as rich or productive as the area around Terry, but the Horseshoe Mining Company had several mines and its large gold mill along upper Whitetail Creek.

2.8 mi **Aztec Hill:** The mountain that US 85/14A tops west of Lead is known as Aztec Hill. It reportedly takes its name from the Golden Reward's Aztec Mine, which sat just west of the highway, near the crest of the hill. The mining company dug a shaft and built a hoist house and several support buildings there in the early twentieth century. The hoist house still stands but is on private land.

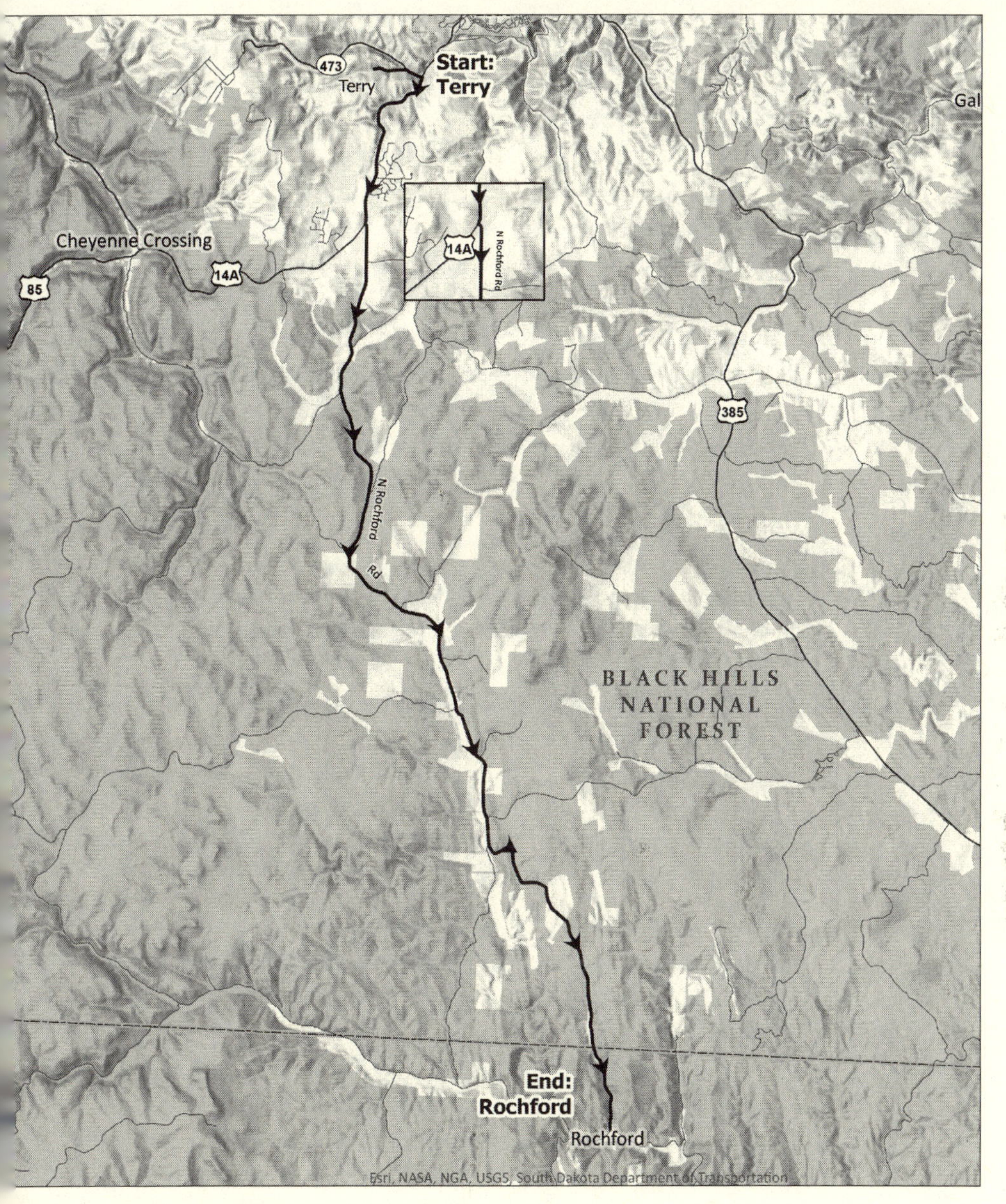
473
Terry
Start:
Terry
Gal
Cheyenne Crossing
85
14A
14A
N Rochford Rd
385
N Rochford
Rd
BLACK HILLS
NATIONAL
FOREST
End:
Rochford
Rochford
Esri, NASA, NGA, USGS, South Dakota Department of Transportation

2.9 mi **Powder House Pass:** To the left (east) is a housing development that takes its name from three large brick buildings the Homestake built to store explosives, primarily dynamite and fuses, in 1919. The Homestake used the powder houses until it turned to a less volatile ammonium nitrate/fuel oil mixture for explosives in the mid-1960s. The BLM currently controls the buildings. They are inaccessible from the road.

The housing development is on land originally owned by the Golden Reward. As the Golden Reward expanded its holdings in the late nineteenth and early twentieth centuries, it acquired much of the land in this area, hoping in vain to find a continuation of the Ruby Basin ore body. The land eventually sold to a development company.

2.9 mi **Deer Mountain Road:** The road that leaves US 85 to the north sits on the roadbed of the Burlington Railroad's Spearfish branch, which operated from 1893 to 1933.

3.6 mi **Junction of US 85/14A and North Rochford Road. Turn left (south) onto North Rochford Road.**

4.0 mi **Brownsville Road, Englewood, Mickelson Trail access:** About a mile east of North Rochford Road on Brownsville Road is Englewood. It once was an important stop on the Burlington Railroad. Today it is home to a trailhead on the Mickelson Trail. Englewood's history is covered in the Northern Black Hills–Homestake Tour.

4.9 mi **Mountain Lawn and Holy Cross Cemeteries:** These two cemeteries were developed next to each other on twenty-five acres of land in 1939. The Catholic Church sponsored Holy Cross, while Lead residents opened the non-sectarian Mountain Lawn.

5.3 mi **Upper Whitewood Creek:** North Rochford Road begins paralleling Whitewood Creek just after it intersects Englewood Road. The creek is very diminutive in this area. Small sections of it can be seen from North Rochford Road. Despite the creek's small size, its drainage provided a path for the Cheyenne-to-Deadwood Trail. Entrepreneurs opened stage stops and roadhouses along the trail, occasionally naming them after the distance to a destination, such as Twenty-Mile Ranch and Ten-Mile Ranch, each marking the distance to Deadwood. Ten-Mile Ranch sat a short distance down Englewood Road. A telegraph line was also built along the wagon road to Deadwood in late 1876.

Like all Black Hills creeks, natural springs feed Whitewood Creek, but its flow has been altered over the years. The Homestake built a system of flumes that captured much of the northern Black Hills spring water, diverting it to Englewood and then to Lead for industrial and domestic use. When the Homestake closed, it turned the waterworks over to the Lead-Deadwood Sanitary District, which still uses it. The original water flumes were made of wood staves, but the district has replaced most of them with modern materials.

8.4 mi **Dumont:** A short distance east of North Rochford Road is Dumont. A large earthen berm crosses the gulch near its location. The Burlington Railroad established Dumont, naming it after Charles Dumont, an early French settler, in 1890. Dumont sat at the highest point on the railroad's main line through the Black Hills, at 6,150 feet (Deadwood, for comparison, is at 4,531 feet). In fact, it was the highest point on the Burlington's entire standard gauge system, although the rail company crossed higher elevations with its narrow gauge tracks in Colorado. With the track going downhill in both directions, the rail company saw Dumont as a place to prepare trains for the downhill trip, especially since the section to Englewood was down a nearly 3.5 percent grade. The railroad also placed a section house and sidings to load timber and cattle at Dumont. Ranchers often used the nearby mountain meadows to pasture their cattle in the summer. The small town that developed had several homes, a school, and a saloon.

The earthen berm carried a railroad spur across the gulch to the Homestake's pump station at Hanna, about four miles to the northwest. The Homestake built the Hanna station in 1900 to pump water out of the Spearfish Creek drainage and over the divide to Englewood for delivery to Lead. The railroad brought in coal for the steam-powered pumps until electric pumps were introduced in 1915. The Homestake also built a small number of employee homes at Hanna. The Lead-Deadwood Sanitary District still uses the pump station, and the Homestake sold the homes.

9.5 mi **Dumont Mickelson Trailhead:** Immediately off the road, to the west, is the Dumont Mickelson Trailhead. Although it is about one mile south of Dumont's actual location, and not quite at the top of the hill, the trailhead was placed here for easy access to North Rochford Road. This location allows snowmobiles to enter the trail and gives bicyclists a place to rest after conquering the uphill climbs.

9.5 mi **Juso Ranch Road:** Across from the Mickelson Trailhead is Juso Ranch Road, named after the family that became famous for building log structures, including Deadwood's rodeo grounds. The Juso family was part of a small Finnish enclave that settled in the area.

Juso Ranch Road leads to the Pathways Spiritual Sanctuary. Black Hills businessman Dave Snyder established the sanctuary in 2010 as a place for people to walk, sit, contemplate, read, write, reflect, or heal.

11.3 mi **Bulldog Ranch:** The white house and outbuildings at the junction of North Rochford and Besant Roads are part of what is known as Bulldog Ranch. Although not a formal stage stop, bullwhackers and travelers on the Cheyenne-to-Deadwood Trail stopped here for food, whiskey, and entertainment. John and Sarah Ann Erb established the ranch about 1878. Mrs. Erb apparently kept two bulldogs to guard her chickens, earning her the nickname "Madame Bulldog." When the Erbs divorced, they sold the stage stop, but it continued to operate and became famous for selling bootleg whiskey.

11.7 mi **North Fork Rapid Creek:** South of Dumont, North Rochford Road parallels the North Fork of Rapid Creek. Just as the Cheyenne-to-Deadwood wagon road followed Whitewood Creek north of Dumont, it paralleled this creek south of Dumont. A small ledge on the hillside to the west once held the historic trail. The trail's route, however, changed over the years, and several locations may be identified with it.

A barn along Rochford Road, sided and shingled with so-called cyanide lids.
South Dakota State Historical Society

12.1 mi **Old Salt Road:** While it is hard to say how this road got its name, it is possible that it came from stories of wagons spilling salt along the road during transport from a manufacturing facility north of Newcastle, Wyoming. The name might also refer to a "crusty" old timer.

12.5 mi **Cyanide lid barn:** Just off the road to the west is a distinctive barn. Its sides and a third of its roof are made of what traditionally have been called cyanide can lids. Structures with similar siding material can be found elsewhere in the Black Hills, but sometimes the supposed cyanide can lids have NaCl (the chemical formula for salt) embossed on them. Salt was in high demand as a food preservative, whereas cyanide was only used in gold mills, so most, if not all, of these lids probably came from salt cans.

13.3 mi **Nahant, near the intersection of Nahant and North Rochford Roads:** The Burlington established Nahant about a half mile south of this location to serve area mines and ranches in 1890. The origins of the name are unknown. It may honor an early French prospector, but more likely it was named after a summer resort near Boston, Massachusetts. Financiers from Boston reportedly had interests in nearby mines. In any case the settlement remained small, and when the McLaughlin Tie & Timber Company opened a sawmill just below where the highway is today, the Burlington relocated Nahant to this location in 1906. McLaughlin Tie & Timber constructed a substantial sawmill complex, and the Burlington built a small depot and service yard. This activity caused the town to boom to 500 residents, with a school, a post office, a hotel, and other businesses.

McLaughlin Tie & Timber: McLaughlin initially supplied ties and bridge materials to the Burlington Railroad in Spearfish Canyon at Savoy in 1892. He then opened logging camps at Elmore, Maurice, and Iron Creek in Spearfish Canyon. When all the harvestable timber in the canyon had been taken, McLaughlin moved operations to Nahant. A pine bark beetle infestation had killed a vast number of trees in the western half of the forest from 1898 to 1908. The Department of Agriculture contracted with him to salvage the usable beetle kill at a minimum price. McLaughlin planned to cut a swath ten miles wide, starting near the Burlington rail line, extending west into Wyoming, and ending near O'Neil Pass, beginning in 1906. To handle the work, he built a thirty-two-mile-long railroad and constructed a sawmill to manufacture ties, poles, and bridge supports. As the beetle killed wood became too porous and brittle, demand fell off, forcing McLaughlin to halt rail operations and to find other sources of timber in 1916. The sawmill continued to operate until 1923. Nahant was abandoned soon after.

Custer bear kill: An avid hunter, during his 1874 Black Hills expedition Colonel George Armstrong Custer fulfilled a lifelong ambition of bagging a grizzly bear. Custer shot the bear twice about a mile and a half south of Nahant. Captain William A. Ludlow, chief of engineers, and Custer's scout Bloody Knife followed up with three more shots. Bloody Knife then slit the animal's throat. No one asked whether Custer's bullets had killed the bear. They all knew it was Custer's bear.

18.0 mi **Rochford Chapel:** The Presbyterian Church authorized a mission chapel at Rochford in the early 1960s. It took a little time for con-

Custer's grizzly bear, bagged south of Custer Peak in 1874. From left to right: Bloody Knife, Colonel Custer, Private Noonan, and Captain Ludlow. *South Dakota State Historical Society*

struction to begin, but once it did, local men did the log work, including the Juso family from Dumont. The chapel's first service was held in June 1966. Catholic and Methodist churches had served Rochford in the early years, but once those had closed, residents used the community hall for services until this chapel was constructed.

18.2 mi **Intersection of North Rochford and Rochford Roads: The tour turns left (east) onto Rochford Road.**

18.5 mi **Mickelson Trailhead at Rochford**

Recommended Rochford Stop: Either stop in downtown Rochford, near the intersection of North Rochford and Rochford Roads, or travel 0.3 miles east on Rochford Road to stop at the Mickelson Trailhead.

Mining and Rochford: This town sits on Rapid Creek. As the creek flows east, its waters are impounded by Pactola Dam. Prospectors identified placer gold in several places along the creek's course, with the Pactola area attracting the most attention. While some placer activity happened around Rochford, this camp owes its existence to hardrock mining. Michael D. Rochford is generally credited with identifying gold outcroppings in its vicinity, and he and Richard B. Hughes founded the town in February 1877. His discoveries naturally attracted other prospectors. Several mines opened, including the King of the West, the Yellow Bird, the Golden West, the Montana, and the Minnesota Ridge. All of them had fairly similar histories. Early success encouraged the owners to build processing plants. At least two large stamp mills were producing gold by 1879, but the low-grade ore failed to pay on a long-term basis. Still, the miners made just enough profit to keep looking, especially when the price of gold rose during the Depression. The 1930s witnessed a flourish of activity as old mine buildings were refurbished and new processing plants went up. The Minnesota Ridge Mine, a few miles northeast of Rochford, gained a small smelter and a new name, Gold Incorporated. Champion boxer Jack Dempsey supposedly backed the venture, but it failed to pay and soon closed.

The Standby Mill at Rochford, 1971. *Watson Parker Ghost Town Notebooks, Leland D. Case Library for Western Historical Studies, Black Hills State University*

Small towns also popped up near the mines, such as Myersville to the west of Rochford and Diamond City to the east. Rochford sat at the center of the action. The Montezuma Mine was north of Rochford, but it had a mill on the town's outskirts. The Standby Mine, just east of town, was the region's most important location, and it attracted plenty of attention. Miners dug open pits, sank a shaft, and pushed a horizontal adit into the mountain. The workings are sealed today, but an airman from Ellsworth AFB died while trying to explore the shaft in 1966. A large, forty-stamp mill was built at the Standby Mine in 1880, and various operators tried running it. In 1936, W. D. Beardshear and his son George remodeled the mill and operated a portion of it until the 1940s. The Homestake explored the property in 1979, thinking the ore resembled what it mined in Lead, but did not find enough to make mining worthwhile.

Mineral Mountain Mining of Canada has recently gained control of several Rochford area claims, believing it can find the wealth that other operators missed. The company was already exploring in the Keystone area when it began acquiring property around Rochford in 2013. It purchased the Standby Mine by 2016. When Mineral Mountain bought it from the Beardshear family, who had held it for over a century, the company promised to name any major discovery after George Beardshear. In total, Mineral Mountain has acquired 7,500 acres between Rapid and Castle Creeks, including many historic mining locations. The company drilled fourteen exploratory holes in 2018, then suspended operations. In August 2020, it applied for a permit to resume drilling directly behind the Standby. Its geologists believe the area contains an extension of the Homestake vein. At one point, they optimistically estimated 268,000 ounces of gold on the property, the estimated equivalent of over $480 million.

The Town of Rochford: Somewhere between 500 and 1,000 people came to town as mining began, with 200 houses and numerous stores, hotels, and saloons going up. Main Street Rochford looked much more substantial than what remains. Several businesses sat across from today's Community Hall. The town never had a major boom, but the recurring efforts to operate the nearby mines kept it viable. In 1880, the census taker counted 315 people, making it the third-largest community in Pennington County, trailing Rockerville by only six people and Rapid City by twenty. Rochford got a boost when the Burlington Railroad built through in 1890, although the railroad put its station and service facilities about a mile east of town. The company claimed that Rochford lacked the space for a small rail yard, but other reasons, such as the price of land, may have played a part. Rochford fell on hard times by the end of the 1890s. Only forty-eight people lived there in 1900.

The federal government helped Rochford when the Forest Service established an office on its outskirts in the early twentieth century, and when the CCC opened a camp about five miles southwest of town in 1933. For one of its projects, the CCC built three homes and an office for the Rochford Ranger Station. The attractive homes were set against the hillside behind the current fire station, east of Rochford. The Forest Service closed the office and dismantled the houses in the early 1970s.

A few residents and many visitors keep the town alive. Travelers especially enjoy two local establishments: the Moonshine Gulch Saloon and the Small of America, a general merchandise store. The saloon got its start when Rochford resident Ted Brown acquired a derelict building which purportedly had housed an early saloon, remodeled it, and opened the new establishment in 1947. The bar's namesake gulch is one mile east of Rochford. Immediately south of the Moonshine Gulch Saloon is a wood frame building that formerly served as the Irish Gulch Dance Hall, named after a gulch that comes into Rochford from the north. At one time a small Irish settlement called the gulch home. A two-story structure that once stood just north of the Moonshine Gulch Saloon had a sign in front claiming that Annie Tallent, of the 1874 Gordon Party, had lived there. After being evicted by the army in 1875, she returned to the Black Hills and lived in a variety of locations. One of those may have been Rochford. Whether she actually lived in the house has been debated, but it became a moot point when the structure burned in 1971. Finally, a group of friends acquired the old Rochford school to use as a summer retreat. They call it the University of Rochford.

Part Fourteen Mystic

Route Overview: From Rochford, travel east on Rochford Road to Mystic Road. Turn right (south) onto Mystic Road. Travel south to George Frink Road. Turn left (east) for a Recommended Stop at the Mystic Mickelson Trailhead.

Mileage starts at Mickelson Trailhead at Rochford.

0.0 mi **Rochford: Depart Mickelson Trailhead and head east on Rochford Road.**

Rapid Creek: For the next 4.3 miles Rochford Road parallels Rapid Creek. Streams from the central Black Hills come together to form the creek. The north and south forks of Rapid Creek converge just west of Rochford. Castle and Slate Creeks join it before it flows into Pactola Dam. Rapid Creek then runs through Rapid City, meeting the Cheyenne River about six miles east of the city. It is one of the Black Hills' main drainages.

0.6 mi **Burlington Section House:** The Burlington Railroad built the house north of the road for the employee who was responsible for the maintenance of this section of track. The railroad also had a station, a water tower, and other support facilities in this area.

1.0 mi **Silver Creek Road:** The Rochford Mining District extended east to Silver Creek. Ore similar to the Standby Mine's had been discovered here in 1879, and several small mines opened. The town of Diamond City also came to life, with a saloon and a dozen houses. The Charter Oak Mine opened the following year, and the camp of Evansville sprang up, named after Evan Evans, one of the mine owners. The mines and towns soon faltered when the gold and silver proved hard to find. Capitalists eventually consolidated most of the claims into the Gordelia Mining Company and built a ten-stamp mill. When it too failed, the Gold King Company took control. More exploration followed, which was also unsuccessful. Ranches and homes have replaced the mines along Silver Creek Road.

Start:
Rochford
Rochford
BLACK HILLS
NATIONAL
FOREST
Rochford Rd
Rochford Rd
Mystic Rd
Mystic Rd
Mystic
End
Myst
Mickelso
Trailhea

1.9 mi **Bloody Gulch Road:** According to *South Dakota Geographic Names*, this gulch was unnamed until an English prospector drank too much water from its small creek. The water carried a heavy mix of minerals, causing the man to become ill. When his associates asked him what was wrong, he replied, "Oh, I drank the water in that bloody gulch!"

4.2 mi **Junction of Rochford and Mystic roads: Turn right (south) onto Mystic Road.** Just after the turn, the road crosses Rapid Creek. This creek has been prospected since the early days of the gold rush, with unremarkable results, but the high price of gold has encouraged recreational placer miners to continue looking. Several claims have been worked near this location.

5.8 mi **Mystic Mining District:** A small mineralized zone starts in this area and extends south for about a mile. A few hardrock mines opened, such as the Cuttysark, in the late nineteenth and early twentieth centuries. None of them produced much ore.

6.6 mi **The Fairview Mine:** The gulch to the right (west) is Pony Gulch. The Fairview Mine, developed in 1880 and operated intermittently, sat a short distance down the gulch. Most notably, the operator of a gold mill at Mystic acquired the Fairview in 1904, hoping it would provide the ore he needed to make a profit (it did not). Still, others tried their luck. The last period of development came in 1937 when a new mill was built, but success again proved elusive. A few scattered ruins remain at the mine site.

6.9 mi **Junction of Mystic Road and George Frink Road: Turn to the left (east) on George Frink Road to Mickelson Trailhead.**

7.2 mi **Recommended Stop at Mystic Mickelson Trailhead:** The trailhead shelter's map of early twentieth century Mystic gives a good overview of this location.

Members of the 1875 Newton–Jenny Expedition camped along Castle Creek.
South Dakota State Historical Society

Castle Creek: Mystic sits on Castle Creek, the third stream in the Black Hills where prospectors found gold, and it seemed to carry more gold than French or Spring Creeks. Castle Creek runs from the western edge of the Black Hills to just below Mystic, where it flows into Rapid Creek. In 1874, the Custer Expedition entered the Black Hills from the west along this creek, and the canyon's high limestone cliffs reminded Custer of castle walls.

When the Newton–Jenney Expedition came through in 1875, they reported finding miners along Castle Creek, and a photographer with the expedition photographed a few of them. General Crook followed Newton and Jenney into the area and removed many of the prospectors as he attempted to uphold the 1868 Fort Laramie Treaty. Of course, these determined people returned a short time later.

Mystic: Originally known as Sitting Bull, this camp took on a variety of roles and had a series of ups and downs over the years. Originally a placer camp, it evolved into a hardrock mining town, a railroad center, a logging camp, and a traveler stop. These economic transformations also caused the center of town to shift; it initially sat along the trail that ran between Hill City and Rochford, which roughly paralleled today's Mystic Road. When the town's focus shifted to hardrock mining, railroading, and logging, most of those activities took place in the valley near the Mickelson Trailhead. The growth of auto travel again made the Mystic Road area the center of attention.

Sitting Bull's Placer Years: The camp came into existence in April 1877, a little later in the rush than most placer towns. Gold was discovered in Castle Creek as early as July 1875, and prospectors established Castleton, a little over a mile above Mystic, in early 1876. While gold could be found near the surface of Castle Creek, however, most of it sat on bedrock buried thirty feet deep. The miners struggled to overcome the depth and the water, and Castleton's population ebbed as the prospectors moved on to easier diggings. Some of them stopped at Sitting Bull. By June 1877, two months after its founding, the new camp reportedly had two dozen log cabins, with twelve serving as homes and twelve as businesses. An entrepreneur named Dr. Burleigh had stimulated much of the growth; to reach the gold, he brought in a crew to dig shafts and install pumps. His operation sat just across the creek from the camp. But the project failed. By 1879, the pumps sat abandoned, and the town was nearly deserted.

Sitting Bull and Hard Rock Mining: Mining men felt sure that the placer gold had come from the neighboring mountains. Their search seemingly paid off when they staked the Fairview claim in Pony Gulch and several other claims in 1880. While these mines produced some gold, none of them were very rich, and they opened and closed repeatedly over the years. At one point, the Fairview Mine owners erected a mill they called the Inca near Castle Creek. Despite the intermittent operations, this activity sufficed to keep Sitting Bull alive.

Railroads and Experimental Gold Plant: Sitting Bull experienced another small boom when the Burlington Railroad built through in 1890. The railroad's arrival meant that people could come and go more easily, and that the nearby mines could secure equipment and supplies at a lower cost. The catch was that the railroad did not like two-word town names, and it changed Sitting Bull to Mystic, after a port town in Connecticut. Despite the rebranding, for a time many people still called it Sitting Bull. The Burlington also took advantage of the small valley just below the original townsite to locate its facilities, causing the town's center to shift.

The railroad access also helped secure an experimental gold processing plant in 1900. Chicago inventor F. H. Long claimed he had discovered an "electro-chemical gold reduction" process that would recover 90 percent of the gold from even the most difficult ores. Long and his backers picked Mystic for their plant because of its rail connection and because of its central location in the Black Hills. They believed that their process would encourage mine owners to ship their ore to the plant from throughout the region. Its construction gave Mystic a boost but provided little sustained benefit. The experimental process did not work as hoped and the ore failed to arrive, preventing the plant from operating continuously. The owners hoped for better days when the Rapid Canyon Line (RCL) arrived in 1906, connecting the facility to Rapid City and potential mineral resources along Rapid Creek. Sadly, the mines produced little wealth, and the plant closed permanently in 1912. It was dismantled and shipped to Glendale, outside of Keystone, for another project Long had started. During the time that the gold plant and the RCL both operated, Mystic's population nearly doubled to 200.

After the gold plant's failure, the Burlington and RCL kept the little town alive. The two railroads interchanged passengers and freight at Mystic, and because the location served as the RCL's end of track, the railroad built a station and a small service yard, including a turntable. The pit for the turntable still exists.

The Frink Family: The gold plant's operation had one lasting impact on the town: it brought William Frink, one of its Chicago backers, to Mystic. The Frink family would stay for nearly a century. William arrived in 1900 and soon became the plant's superintendent. As the operation struggled, he began repurposing the facilities. In 1903, he converted the company's boarding house into a resort, hoping to attract travelers who wished to rest and fish. He also turned the company commissary into a small grocery store. Six years after the gold plant's removal, two timber men, Savage and Sanford, along with

The Frink Sawmill near Mystic, 1926. *Black Hills National Forest Historical Collection, Leland D. Case Library for Western Historical Studies, Black Hills State University*

George Frink, William's son, erected a sawmill on the mill's foundations. George took sole charge of the operation in 1919 and ran it until 1952. With the sawmill and two railroads providing employment, about thirty families lived in the area in 1939.

When automobiles started traveling from Hill City to Rochford along Mystic Road, George and his brother, William Jr., decided to capitalize on the town's improved accessibility. William Jr. built a grocery store, a garage, an icehouse, and a chicken coop on the east side of the road, and a home on the west side, across from the store. George also constructed six tourist cabins on a hillside above town. Soon after, Oscar Donaldson, a Presbyterian missionary, raised funds to build the McCahan Memorial Chapel, just below the William Frink house, naming it after the largest benefactor.

The Depression era's higher gold prices brought a small boom to Mystic. Placer miners came back and the Fairview Mine produced a small amount of gold. The economic boost would soon fade, and Mystic struggled in the years following World War II. The RCL closed in 1947; the sawmill shut down in 1952. The consequent decline left only a few residents, including the Frink family. The Mystic townsite had never been filed, meaning that the residents had to sign leases with the Forest Service to live there. In 1985, the Forest Service supervisor began canceling the leases. The Frink family, with the help of the Historic South Dakota Foundation, got the Mystic townsite designated as an historic district in 1986. Russell Frink, George's son, was allowed to remain as the district's caretaker. When his house mysteriously burned in 1995, he too left. Today, only the assay office and the gold mill's foundations remain in the lower part of Mystic, near the Mickelson Trailhead, while the chapel, a garage, and a home sit along Mystic Road.

Part Fifteen Mystic to Hill City

Route Overview: From the Mystic Trailhead return to Mystic Road. After Mystic Road merges with Deerfield Road, continue to Hill City.

Mileage starts at Mickelson Trailhead at Mystic.

0.0 mi **Mystic: Return to Mystic Road.**

0. 2 mi **George Frink Road and Mystic Road intersection: Turn left (south) onto Mystic Road.**

1.6 mi **Castleton Dredge:** Castle Creek was known for deep gold, an estimated twenty to thirty feet below the surface. To reach it, in 1911 Denver financiers brought in a bucket-line dredge to scoop out the overburden. For a time, the dredge operated twenty-four hours a day. A newspaper reported that it found a large amount of gold, but a very jagged and uneven rock bottom made operations difficult. The paper speculated that there might have been only one "rich spot" in the creek. It may have been right, as further efforts produced little gold.

The Castleton Dredge, ca. 1912–1914. *South Dakota State Historical Society*

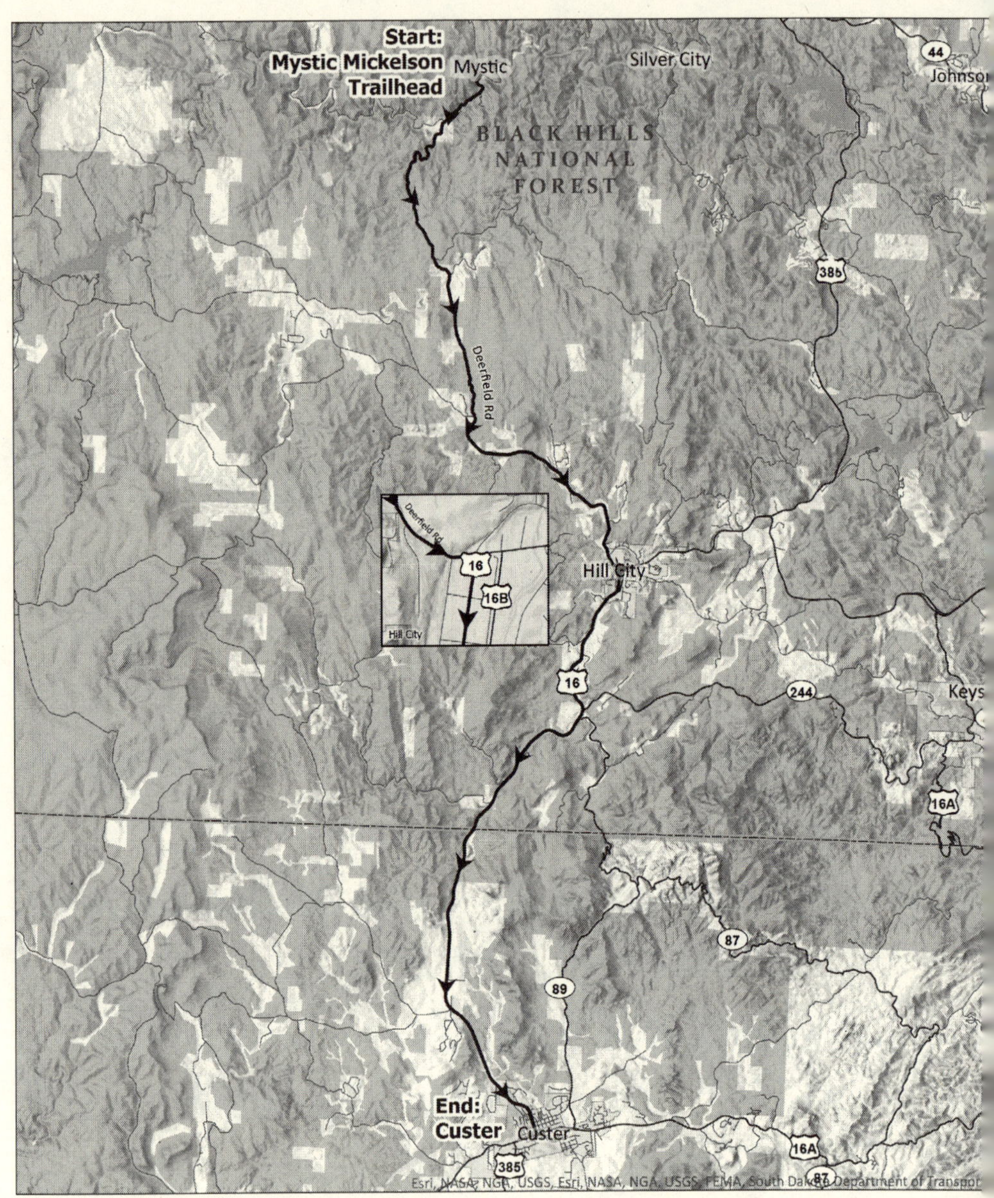
Start:
Mystic Mickelson
Trailhead
Mystic
Silver City
44
Johnson
BLACK HILLS
NATIONAL
FOREST
385
Deerfield Rd
Deerfield Rd
16
16B
Hill City
Hill City
16
244
Keys
16A
87
89
End:
Custer
Custer
385
16A
87
Esri, NASA, NGA, USGS, Esri, NASA, NGA, USGS, FEMA, South Dakota Department of Transport

The operators shut down the dredge in 1915 and sold it to a company in Oregon. The ribs of the barge that kept it afloat can still be seen in the southernmost pond when the water level is low. Piles of rock along the creek indicate where the dredge operated.

1.7 mi **Castle Creek and Castleton:** Prospectors who returned to the Castle Creek area after being removed by General Crook in 1875 established the town of Castleton at this location. It quickly swelled to 250 people, with about forty or fifty cabins. The bedrock, however, proved too deep for effective gold recovery, and the miners left.

When the Burlington Railroad built through in 1890, crews had to drill two tunnels in the mountainside just east of Castle Creek. To house the workers, the company established a construction camp at Castleton, bringing new life to the area. Once the tunnels were completed, the workers moved on.

Lookout Mine: Castle Creek also had hardrock mining. The Lookout Mine was located about three miles west of Castleton. Discovered in 1882, it was named for its location high on the mountainside. The owners built a large stamp mill and developed a town, named Lookout, that reportedly grew to 600. As elsewhere, the mine and town quickly faded.

Deerfield Dam: When the federal government decided to irrigate Rapid Valley and create work during the Depression, it envisioned building two dams in the Black Hills, Deerfield on Castle Creek and Pactola on Rapid Creek. While Pactola Dam was delayed until the 1950s, work went ahead on Deerfield Dam. The Farm Security Administration and the CCC started the project in 1939. When the onset of World War II siphoned off manpower, the CCC program ended and the government assigned conscientious objectors to the job. The Bureau of Reclamation ultimately finished the 835-foot-long earthen dam, creating a 414-acre lake, in 1947. Deerfield Dam is located about eight miles west of Castleton.

5.4 mi **Horse Creek Road:** Slate Creek, a tributary of Rapid Creek, is accessed by Horse Creek Road. Early reports said that Native peoples followed Rapid Creek and then Slate Creek into the Black Hills. Travelers frequently commented on seeing either Indians or their trails in the area.

Slate Creek Dam: Slate Creek Dam is about three miles down Horse Creek Road. The Warren-Lamb Lumber Company of Rapid City built the first Slate Creek Dam to provide water for a six-mile-long wooden flume used to transport logs to the railroad in Rapid Canyon. The company used the flume from 1920 to 1924 but encountered a variety of problems that kept the flume from working satisfactorily, such as too little water during dry periods. The company abandoned the dam, but the CCC rebuilt it in 1936.

Besides constructing the dam, Warren-Lamb also carved a rock tunnel for the flume farther down Slate Creek. Because someone has installed what appear to be bunkbeds in the tunnel, it has become known as the Miner's Hotel. ATV/UTV riders visit it frequently.

7.0 mi **Redfern:** To the left (east) is a derelict railroad car sitting in a field. It marks the location of a small town known as Redfern. The Mickelson Trail also has a shelter and interpretative sign near the townsite. Redfern, named after an employee, Albert Redfern, was the creation of the Burlington Railroad. Initially a construction camp, it became a small service center. The remaining rail car served as a section house for employees. In the 1950s, the Black Hills Silica Sand Corporation built a processing plant here. It used area quartz and pegmatite deposits to produce a high-quality sand used in paints, ceramics, and sand blasting. Foundations of the mill can still be found near the Mickelson Trail.

8.8 mi **Mystic Road joins Deerfield Road.**

8.8 mi **Tigerville, sometimes called Tiger City:** The town of Tigerville was located near the junction of Deerfield and Mystic Roads. It came to life around 1877 as miners returned from the northern Black Hills to look for hardrock outcroppings. This town apparently got its name from a series of nearby claims known as the Lucky Tiger. Other mines in the area included the King Solomon and the Bengal

Tiger or Royal Bengal Tiger. The name came from rust streaks on the ore, which resembled tiger stripes. Despite reports of great finds and large payouts, the mines had little value, and no production records can be found. The town apparently hung on into the 1880s with the usual mix of gold town businesses. An estimated 200 people lived there in 1879. An historical marker at the junction of Deerfield and Mystic Roads once noted Tigerville's location, but it disappeared over forty years ago.

10.9 mi **Newton Fork and Newton Lake:** It is believed that Newton Fork, a tributary of Spring Creek, was named for Henry Newton of the 1875 Newton–Jenney Expedition that explored the Black Hills, looking for gold and other resources. Hill City was established near the confluence of Newton Fork and Spring Creek. The CCC constructed Newton Lake in 1934.

11.4 mi **Burnt Fork Road, Gold Mountain Mine:** The Gold Mountain Mine lies 1.8 miles down Burnt Fork Road. Originally known as the Gold Hill group, the property was first explored in the 1920s when prospectors dug a ninety-five-foot shaft, trenches, and shallow open cuts. Despite assays showing nearly a third of an ounce of gold per ton, little mining was done. The Gold Mountain Mining Company leased the property in the 1930s, sank a 170-foot shaft, and built a twenty-five-ton concentrating mill, which it expanded to seventy-five tons in 1938–1940. Forest Service information states that the mine closed in 1942 when the government suspended gold mining, but it appears to have ceased operations prior to that time. In any case, there is no record of production, and no work has been done since 1940.

The headframe, tramway, and hoist house stood until about 1990, when vandals and time took their toll. The Black Hills National Forest Service evaluated the site in 2007 and deemed it a safety hazard, which generally warrants removal and reclamation. Instead of letting that happen, the Black Hills Historic Preservation and Trust Society decided to save what remained. Since the site was on public land, the group worked with the Forest Service to stabilize and interpret it. The preservation society also sought supporters. Jon Crane created a painting that highlighted the boilers, and the Deadwood

Remnants of the Gold Mountain Mine, 2011. *Author photo*

Historic Preservation Commission provided a $40,000 grant. From 2009 to 2013, volunteer and youth groups, including students from the Boxelder Job Corps Civilian Conservation Center, successfully preserved the site. The Forest Service describes it as the "only gold mining site on the BHNF with a standing mill frame."

13.3 mi **Wade's Gold Mill:** This former tourist attraction got its start when Les and Idella Wade built a small mill to concentrate placer gravel in 1979. They soon realized that people were curious about their operation, and they opened Wade's Gold Mill for tours in the early 1980s. Over the next few years, they added historic mining equipment often salvaged from nearby abandoned mines. Visitors could pan for gold and learn about mining history. A highlight was the one-stamp mill that the Wades occasionally operated. The attraction closed after the Wades passed away.

13.6 mi **Marshall Gulch:** Prospectors diligently searched the Hill City area looking for gold without finding much. George Coats, however, located the Sunnyside Mine in Marshall Gulch, named for local miner Ben Marshall, in 1895. Reports state that the mine produced $25,000 in gold, but water problems closed it by 1898.

14.1 mi **Junction of Deerfield Road and US 16/385 in Hill City: Turn right (south) and return to Custer.**

Conclusion A Gold Rush Paradigm
The Black Hills as a Case Study

The Gold Rush Tour has provided a location-by-location overview of mining in the Black Hills. Nearly every place this tour visited included a mining story: the discovery of gold, the founding of a gold camp, and the success or failure of hardrock mining. Even when auxiliary enterprises were discussed, such as lumbering or railroading, they were generally connected to mining. As mentioned in the Introduction, this location-based approach emphasizes the importance of place and the "layers" of history. The disadvantage is that the "big picture" can become lost. In other words, underlying themes or trends can be overwhelmed by details. In truth, many of these locations had common experiences. The Black Hills Gold Rush followed the pattern of other gold rushes in the United States, and so an analysis of the Black Hills can serve as a case study for understanding gold rushes in general. This gold rush paradigm has five parts: 1) discovery and rush, 2) finding a paying location, 3) the search for quartz, 4) the search continues, and 5) the modern era of mining.

The first step, of course, is discovery, which is quickly followed by a rush. In the Black Hills, Horatio Ross and William McKay discovered gold along French Creek during the 1874 Custer Expedition. Custer's dispatch of scout Charley Reynolds to spread the word ignited the rush. Prospectors needed more than just the allure of gold, however, before they would venture their time, energy, and capital. The Panic of 1873 provided that incentive. The resulting economic depression had taken a heavy toll on the nation's farmers, merchants, and laborers, persuading them to try their luck in a distant stream. Prospecting expeditions formed in towns around the Black Hills, such as Cheyenne, Wyoming, and Sioux City, Iowa, but these groups ran into problems. The Lakotas did not want whites invading their homeland, and in accordance with the Fort Laramie Treaty of 1868, the U.S. Army tried to keep out trespassers. Some gold seekers, such as the Gordon Party, still made it to the Black Hills. The army eventually removed these adventurers, but despite patrolling the trails and arresting those who made it into the Hills, as many as 1,500 gold seekers worked the Black Hills' streams in the summer of 1875. The futility of keeping the region closed persuaded President Ulysses S. Grant to withdraw the troops in late 1875, unofficially opening the Black Hills to all.

With French Creek heralded as the discovery site, most early prospectors headed there. Finding the diggings crowded and the gold sparse, many began to look elsewhere and discovered gold on Spring, Rapid, and Castle Creeks. Wherever they went, a small boomtown followed, starting with Custer City on French Creek, then Hill City and Golden City (Sheridan) on Spring Creek, Camp Crook (Pactola) on Rapid Creek, and Castleton on Castle Creek. Catering to a rough-and-tumble clientele, saloons dominated the small business districts. Since their survival depended on the gold content in the adjacent creeks, the camps' existence was tenuous. Just like French Creek, most Black Hills creeks carried limited amounts of gold. Some hotspots certainly existed, such as at Stand-off Bar on Spring Creek, but on the whole, most prospectors walked away disappointed, often failing to find enough gold to pay expenses. The difficulty of the trip, the rigors of camp life, and the lack of gold persuaded many would-be millionaires to return home. While a gold rush implies people continuously arriving, just as many left.

With such meager returns through most of 1875, the gold rush could have ended just as quickly as it had begun. Many of the miners would have left, leaving little lasting impression on the Black Hills. The region's history would have certainly been different. To sustain the gold rush, prospectors needed to find what was known as a paying location, where they made more money per day than they could make working as a laborer. Discovering a paying location would turn the rush from a purely speculative adventure into one offering a real possibility of attaining wealth. Finding a paying location, then, is the second step of the gold rush paradigm.

While some disagreement exists regarding who made the first discovery in Deadwood Gulch, the Lardner Party certainly uncovered paying quantities of gold along Deadwood Creek in November 1875. After the discovery of gold on French Creek in 1874, this was the next most important event of the Black Hills Gold Rush—it proved that real wealth existed in the Hills, and it brought the possibility of permanent settlements and development. As word of the Deadwood Gulch discoveries spread, miners abandoned their claims elsewhere in the Black Hills and headed toward the new diggings, creating the gold camp of Deadwood in April 1876. As the news spread across the nation, more people headed to the new boomtown. Some had no intention of digging in the dirt. Instead, they shrewdly planned to separate the men from their money or "mine the miners" by opening businesses, such as saloons, dance halls, and brothels. As Deadwood boomed, other Black Hills gold camps became ghost towns.

The third step in the gold rush paradigm is the search for quartz. Prospectors initially searched the creeks for placer deposits, or small pieces of loose gold that had settled on the bedrock below a creek bed. Experienced miners knew that the placer deposits had eroded from an outcropping of gold ore, most often occurring as a mixture of gold and quartz. Water not only freed the gold from the quartz, but it also carried the metal to the creeks. After locating placer deposits, prospectors next searched the mountainsides above the creeks for quartz outcroppings.

Fred and Moses Manuel, along with two partners, identified the mountains above Bobtail Gulch, a feeder to Deadwood Gulch, as the likely source of the latter's placer gold. They searched the area throughout early 1876, finding some promising prospects. On 9 April 1876, having finally identified a large ore body, they staked the Homestake Claim. Their work attracted the attention of California mining man George Hearst and his partners, who purchased the Homestake Claim, created the Homestake Mining Company, acquired neighboring claims, and brought in the equipment needed to develop the Black Hills' largest and most important mine.

The region around Deadwood Gulch and the Homestake Mine boomed in 1876–1877. More people poured in and more camps developed, including Lead City and Central City, but the new arrivals found most of the valuable mining ground taken. Good placer and hardrock deposits existed in a relatively small area. Although frustrated, the prospectors felt sure that rich deposits must exist elsewhere in the Black Hills and were simply waiting to be found. Armed with this belief, they revisited the mining grounds recently abandoned in the central and southern Black Hills, bringing new life to Custer City, Hill City, Sheridan, and Pactola. Not only did old locations come back to life, but prospectors made new finds and created new towns, including Rochford on Rapid Creek and Rockerville near Spring Creek. The Keystone and Holy Terror hardrock mines in Keystone proved to be two of the more important discoveries that came with the renewed prospecting. This pursuit of new wealth is the fourth step in the gold rush paradigm, described as "the search continues."

Beyond discovering new gold deposits, miners also looked for other ways to make money. For instance, some mining men realized that new processing techniques could increase gold production. Prospectors had found gold in the Ruby Basin and Bald Mountain Mining Districts west of Lead early in the rush, but it was chemically bound to the rock and could not be recovered with standard milling methods. This forced mining promoters to search for new ways to handle the ore. They eventually adopted smelting and chlorination, and they built plants in lower Deadwood in the late 1880s. Later, the cyanide process would prove even more effective at recovering gold. The success of these methods encouraged the development of new mines and new companies, including the Golden Reward Mining Company, and the creation of new towns such as Terry and Trojan.

Part of the prospectors' ongoing search involved looking for other metals. Though not as valuable as gold, silver had made mine owners wealthy in other western mineral districts, such as at the Comstock Lode in Nevada. Miners never found a large amount of silver in the Black Hills, but they still uncovered enough to cause some excitement and spawn the towns of Galena and Carbonate. Outside of precious metals, prospectors occasionally looked for base metals such as copper and tin, but none existed in marketable quantities. Still, promoters persuaded gullible investors that a large amount of tin existed around Black Elk (Harney) Peak. Since all the tin used in the United States came from England, these reported discoveries promised great returns. It soon became apparent, however, that the Harney Peak Tin Company was a stock scam. The company produced little tin while it swindled millions of dollars from investors. Nevertheless, Hill City benefitted from a new round of construction. The search for tin coincided with miners digging for pegmatites, such as feldspar and mica. While not nearly as valuable as gold or silver, these minerals helped sustain Custer and Keystone after gold mining ended.

Most of the region's gold mines, except the Homestake, closed with the onset of World War I. In 1879, with gold serving as the basis of the nation's monetary system, the federal government had set the price for an ounce of gold at $20.67. Wartime inflation drove up the cost of supplies and labor to the point that making a profit became nearly impossible. During the Great Depression, the Roosevelt administration raised the price of gold to $35 an ounce, encouraging a new generation of prospectors to search creek beds, while hardrock claim holders either redeveloped their old mines or opened new ones. These activities included the reconditioning of the large mill at the Standby Mine in Rochford and the sinking of a shaft and the construction of several buildings at the Gold Mountain Mine north of Hill City. The chance for higher profits also encouraged the Homestake Mine to dig new shafts and to expand its milling facilities.

By the twentieth century, most gold deposits had been discovered and the best methods for mining and milling gold had been pretty well established. Where new mining and milling techniques had once been the crucial factors in advancing the industry, the price of gold had now become the key to bringing changes to what can be called the modern era of mining, the fifth step in the gold rush paradigm. After the price advance during the Depression, gold remained at $35 an ounce until the government let the market dictate the price in the 1970s. When the value of gold sharply increased, the Homestake Mining Company expanded operations, and other companies acquired long-abandoned properties to open mines, such as the Gilt Edge near Galena, the Golden Reward in the Ruby Basin District, and the Wharf in the Bald Mountain District.

The year 2024 marks the 150th anniversary of the onset of the gold rush with Ross and McKay's discovery in 1874. Much has changed over the intervening years, but the fact remains that the search for gold only enriched a few. The vast majority of prospectors found nothing and left the Black Hills deeper in debt than when they arrived. Moreover, when mining companies took control of the best mines, only small amounts of wealth stayed in the region. Most of the profits flowed to stockholders in California and elsewhere. Nevertheless, towns such as Lead and Deadwood benefitted from the wages the companies paid and the money they invested in the communities. Other gold rush towns disappeared. Those that survive, including Custer, Keystone, Hill City, Lead, and Deadwood, now rely on other industries, especially tourism, for their economic support. Over the years, the ruins of the old mines have slowly disappeared. Although few physical reminders still exist, the Gold Rush shaped the course of Black Hills history, and mining will continue to play a role in the region's future.

Bibliography

Developing tours that visit and discuss numerous locations and topics requires a wide variety of sources, but since the information is meant for a general audience, I have opted not to provide traditional endnote-style citations. Instead, this bibliography gives an overview of the most important sources I consulted and provides some direction as to where one might look to find more information about Black Hills history.

The notion of developing Black Hills history tours did not originate with this guide. At least four publications already exist that can help a traveler navigate the region's past. In the 1930s, the Works Progress Administration hired unemployed writers to describe the history and culture of each state. The results of this effort, known as the Federal Writers' Project, include *A South Dakota Guide*. It comprises fifteen statewide tours, with the Black Hills mentioned in six. The South Dakota Guide Commission originally published the book in 1938, but it has since been republished, with the South Dakota State Historical Society Press releasing a version in 2005. Leland D. Case, the noted western historian and benefactor to the Case Library for Western Historical Studies at Black Hills State University, published *Lee's Official Guidebook to the Black Hills and the Badlands* (1953). Although Case covered the region in just over 100 pages, he still incorporated much interesting information, dedicating about one page to each of the larger communities. Finally, the "dean" of Black Hills history, Watson Parker, produced two useful books. For several years, Parker and his father, Troy, ran a guest ranch at Palmer Gulch, not far from Mount Rushmore. To help his guests navigate the region, Parker produced the *Palmer Gulch Lodge Guide to the Black Hills* (1960). More importantly, after countless hours locating and researching ghost towns, he and Hugh K. Lambert published *Black Hills Ghost Towns* (1974). The book lists and briefly describes around 600 locations, but because of the way it is organized, *Black Hills Ghost Towns* is difficult to use as a tour guide. Each listing includes a range, township, and section number, but since the towns are listed alphabetically, it is difficult to connect the locations. Moreover, all the publications mentioned above provide only limited information, and they are now quite dated.

For a person interested in learning more about Black Hills history in general, there are several books available. Luckily, many people who arrived with the gold rush wrote down what they saw and heard. Pioneer chronicles include Peter Rosen, *Pa-Ha-Sa-Pah: Or the Black Hills of South Dakota* (1895); Richard B. Hughes, *Pioneer Years in the Black Hills* (1957); John S. McClintock, *Pioneer Days in the Black Hills* (1939); Jesse Brown and A. M. Willard, *The Black Hills Trails* (1924); and Annie D. Tallent, *The Black Hills, or, The Last Hunting Ground of the Dakotahs* (1899). All of these provide valuable insights into Black Hills history, but each has a different focus. For instance, McClintock has seventy-one brief chapters, each covering a distinct topic, from murders to sawmills. While informative, this format makes it difficult to get a good overview of the region's history. Brown and Willard have excellent information on early violence, but the broader aspects of settlement are generally ignored. Tallent's book gives the best summary of early Black Hills history, and people who study the region frequently rely on her, but she includes some incorrect information, and she has been critiqued for her insensitivity toward the American Indian population.

With the assistance of the above sources, several authors have produced good syntheses of Black Hills history, but only three will be mentioned. Watson Parker's *Gold in the Black Hills* (1966) is a must-read for anyone interested in the region's past. Parker not only covers the big events, such as the Custer Expedition and the discovery of gold, but he also discusses the creation of towns, Indigenous-white relations, mining camp violence, and more. The Parker book also has a good bibliography that Black Hills researchers will find useful. Another good synthesis is *Gold, Gals, Guns, Guts* (1976), edited by Bob Lee, with the assistance of Stan Lindstrom and Wynn Lindstrom. Although focused on the northern Black Hills, the book gives a good summary of that region's past and brings the story up to 1976. Finally, journalist Robert J. Casey wrote an engaging monograph emphasizing excitement, titled *The Black Hills and Their Incredible Characters* (1949). Casey, however, needs to be used carefully; he includes stories that he heard without double-checking them for accuracy.

If one desires more information on a specific subject, several publications exist. Four motifs frequently appear in this tour guide: military expeditions, transportation, mining, and town development. Of the military expeditions that visited the Black Hills, the Gold Rush Tour mentions four: Lieutenant Warren's Army Corps of Topographical Engineers survey of 1857, the Custer Expedition of 1874, the Newton–Jenney geological survey of 1875, and General Crook's 1875 effort to remove trespassing miners. From 1973 to 1974, *South Dakota History*, the quarterly journal of the South Dakota State Historical Society, published five articles by James D. McLaird and Lesta V. Turchen titled "Exploring the Black Hills, 1855–1875: Reports of the Government Expeditions." These articles reprinted excerpts from the Warren through the Custer Expeditions. Since Crook's trip into the Black Hills in 1875 did not involve exploration, McLaird and Turchen did not cover it. Information on Crook in the Black Hills can be found in Paul Magid's *The Gray Fox: George Crook and the Indian Wars* (2015). More details about the Newton–Jenney Expedition are available in the journals of Colonel Richard Irving Dodge, who chronicled the adventure while leading the military column that escorted the scientists. Published accounts include Colonel Dodge's *The Black Hills* (1965) and Wayne R. Kime's *The Black Hills Journals of Colonel Richard Irving Dodge* (1996). Because of Custer's notoriety and the repercussions of his 1874 Black Hills expedition, several books mention him and his trip. The most thorough account is Ernest Grafe and Paul Horsted, *Exploring with Custer: The 1874 Black Hills Expedition* (2002, revised 2023). A much smaller but still valuable look at the expedition is Donald Jackson's *Custer's Gold: The United States Cavalry Expedition of 1874* (1966).

Transportation, including wagons and railroads, was important to the development of the Black Hills. The first significant gold rush trail came out of Cheyenne. Agnes Wright Spring's *The Cheyenne and Black Hills Stage and Express Routes* (1948) provides much information about early stagecoach operations. Other trails soon developed, and local historians have produced works for nearly every one, such as Vernon S. Holst's *A Study of the 1876 Bismarck to Deadwood Trail* (1983) and Jan Cerney's *The Fort Pierre-Deadwood Gold Trail* (2006). A few studies give overviews of the trails, including Hyman Palais's "A Study of the Trails to the Black Hills Gold Fields," in *South Dakota Historical Col-*

lections, XXV (1951), and Irma H. Klock's *All Roads Lead to Deadwood* (1979). More information about trails and stagecoach operations can be found by visiting relevant websites. For instance, the Wyoming State Preservation Office has a site titled the "Cheyenne-Black Hills Stage Route Historic District," (wyoshpo.wyo.gov). Two authors provide thorough overviews of the construction and operation of Black Hills' rail lines. Mildred Fielder published "Railroads of the Black Hills" in *South Dakota Historical Collections,* XXX (1960), which she turned into a book, with many more photographs, in 1964. Railroad historian Rick Mills has written about South Dakota railroads in general, and he focused on the Black Hills in at least two publications. His most detailed effort is *125 Years of Black Hills Railroading* (2004).

Several sources are useful in learning about the region's mining past. Contemporaneous newspapers are invaluable. Since much of the region's economy depended on mining, newspapers often covered mining developments in detail. The most useful papers include Deadwood's *Black Hills Daily Times* and *Black Hills Pioneer,* although every Black Hills paper carried mining news, and most of them are available online. Several organizations, such as railroads, published books and brochures that promoted mining investments. One of the most useful came from the Black Hills Mining Men's Association, titled *The Black Hills Illustrated* (1904). Its intent was to encourage investment in underdeveloped mines, but it also contains much good information about the Black Hills in general. The South Dakota School of Mines was another source of mining news. For a time, it produced a regular publication that highlighted mining, although it also carried other Black Hills stories. It went by three names over the years: the *Aurum,* the *PaHaSaPa Quarterly,* and the *Black Hills Engineer.* On a national level, the *Engineering and Mining Journal* regularly carried Black Hills mining news and occasionally ran feature stories. Since the days of the 1857 Warren Expedition, the federal government has taken an interest in the Black Hills' mineral wealth, and that has continued through the years, resulting in publications that are helpful when exploring mining history. In particular, the Bureau of Mines produced two invaluable pieces. One is the *Black Hills Mineral Atlas, Part 1 and Part 2* (1954). These volumes list and briefly discuss every mine and mineral deposit that has been explored, developed, or located. They are a good starting point for understanding the extent and variety of mining activities. The other Bureau of Mines publication is Paul T. Allsman's *Reconnaissance of Gold-Mining Districts in the Black Hills, S. Dak.* (1940). While not as comprehensive as the *Mineral Atlas*, it provides more detailed information on the important mining companies.

Several authors with Black Hills' connections have also published books related to mining history. Mildred Fielder lived in Lead, and two of her publications focus on mining: *Silver is the Fortune* (1978) and *A Guide to Black Hills Ghost Mines* (1972). The former looks at the silver camps of Galena and Carbonate, with an emphasis on their mining past, and the latter discusses over twenty mines, including how to find them. Many of the mines have unfortunately disappeared since the book came out. Another local author, Irma H. Klock, specialized in pamphlet-length publications, and two of them look at mining towns and their adjacent mines: *Yesterday's Gold Camps and Mines in the Northern Black Hills* (1975) and *The Central Black Hills* (1986). Joel Waterland, a Homestake Mining Company geologist, wrote three books on mines in the northern Black Hills: *The Spawn & the Mother Lode* (1987), *Gold & Silver or Sweat & Tears* (1988), and *The Mines Around & Beyond* (1991). Waterland filled these books with details, which can make them difficult to read. Finally, the Homestake Mine is a big part of Black Hills mining history, and several authors have examined its past. One of the most informative books is by Steven T. Mitchell, a longtime Homestake employee, titled *Nuggets to Neutrinos: The Homestake Story* (2009). Another excellent book about the mine is William Bronson and T. H. Watkins, *Homestake: The Centennial History of America's Greatest Gold Mine* (1977).

Information about the towns and locations the tour visits came from a variety of sources. Many mining history books include information about the adjacent towns, and a few of the authors mentioned above have written specifically about mining camps. For instance, Klock looked at the communities along Deadwood Creek in *The Gold Camps in Upper Deadwood Gulch* (1984). Local writers have also produced several books about their hometowns or about a town that interests them, such as Linda Sandness, Colleen Langley, and Lauree Oerlline Buus, *Rochford: The Friendliest Little Ghost Town in the Black Hills* (2013), and Alice Davis Smith, *Lowdown on Hilltown: Historical Annals of Hill City, South Dakota* (2002). Martha Linde of Custer discussed seven central Black Hills towns in *Rushmore's Golden Valleys* (1976). Besides the published material, some communities provide good local histories through websites and walking tours. Keystone, for instance, provides the Historic Keystone Walking Tour. Some towns have historic buildings or districts listed on the National Register of Historic Places, and in those instances, accessing the nomination forms can prove worthwhile. An online search can help identify properties listed on the register, and the South Dakota State Historic Preservation Office in Pierre can also be helpful. Sometimes the nominations are printed and available at area archives and libraries, such as Robert G. Rosenberg's 1985 study, "Mystic Townsite Historic District Nomination and Historic Report." A good source on just about every Black Hills location is Watson Parker's Ghost Town Notebooks, held at the Case Library for Western Historical Studies in Spearfish. These notebooks contain the research that Parker spent a lifetime gathering to produce *Black Hills Ghost Towns*. Other sources that should not be ignored include county history books, such as *Some History of Lawrence County* (1981) and the popular publication, *South Dakota Magazine*. This periodical occasionally highlights a Black Hills community.

In closing, there are many locations a researcher can find information, and perhaps the easiest place to start is online. The U.S. Forest Service, local businesses, tourist attractions, South Dakota Public Broadcasting, and outdoor recreation groups have websites that can provide good introductions to a topic or location. A web search may also identify relevant articles that have appeared in scholarly journals, such as *South Dakota History*. In total, there are many possible sources, and in putting this tour together, I checked most of them.

Index